THE
YOUNG
AMERICAN'S
UNOFFICIAL
GUIDE TO THE
VERY BRITISH
WORLD
OF

Harry Potter

VOLUME
ONE

Also by Dana Middleton

The Infinity Year of Avalon James

Open If You Dare

The Young American's Unofficial Guide to the Very British World of Harry Potter

VOLUME ONE

DANA MIDDLETON

SHADOWRIDGE PRESS

THE YOUNG AMERICAN'S UNOFFICIAL GUIDE
TO THE VERY BRITISH WORLD
OF HARRY POTTER

First published February 2019
by Shadowridge Press

Book design by Robert Barr.

ISBN: 978-1-946808-14-1

shadowridgepress.com

"The United States and Great Britain are two nations separated by a common language"

— *variously attributed to George Bernard Shaw, Oscar Wilde, & Winston Churchill*

CONTENTS

WHAT THIS BOOK IS ABOUT
AND HOW TO USE IT

Imagine a world without Harry Potter. If you're a reader of the Harry Potter books, you know that's simply impossible. Because once you've opened your heart to Harry's amazing and magical world, there's no going back.

Some books capture the public's imagination in a way that others never do. Although written for children, J.K. Rowling's Harry Potter books speak to all of us, at all ages. Although I am years older than my nieces and nephews, I could swear we are the same age whenever we talk about Harry, Ron and Hermione. These characters are alive for us. They've become our friends and we love to talk about them with each other. I suspect we aren't the only ones who share this experience.

But when I first read *Harry Potter and the Sorcerer's Stone*, I became aware of lots of words, phrases and other references that are distinctly British and may be hard for most of us Americans to understand (even though the language of the American Editions has been edited to be more accessible to us). As I progressed through the books, I felt that Americans might be missing out on some of the richness and cleverness of J.K. Rowling's wonderful writing because of certain linguistic and cultural differences between us and the British.

Many of the words that J.K. Rowling uses to tell her stories are foreign to us. Especially the slang words. Tell me honestly, had you ever heard the words 'git' or 'crikey' before Harry Potter? And when was the last time you ate a shepherd's pie or a knickerbocker glory? And have any of you ever ridden on the Underground or watched a fireworks celebration on Bonfire Night? It's like I'm speaking a different language, right? And the list goes on and on.

That's why I decided to write this book. To explain all of the British words and phrases along with some cultural, geographical and historical references that appear in the Harry Potter books that might be alien to most Americans.

At this point, you might be wondering why I (an American) am qualified to take you on this journey of translation and revelation. The answer is simple. Along with my American nieces and nephews, I have an English niece, too. You see, I am married to an Englishman named Pete and ever since, a magical world has been opened up to me. I'm not talking about Harry Potter's wizarding world. I'm talking about his British one.

My experiences with Pete and his family and friends have given me a unique view of British people, culture and history. They have taught me so many things—from outrageously fun slang words to how to make a Christmas pudding—all of which I will be sharing with you in the following pages.

Here's how this book works. We are going to use the Harry Potter books as our starting point to learn more about that fascinating foreign world in which Harry and his friends live. We will explore the meanings of the words that are unknown to us, plus some that aren't so unknown but could use further explanation. Also, we'll take what I hope is an interesting and humorous look into some of Britain's history and culture.

This is Volume One of the series. I'll go through the books sequentially starting, in this volume, with *Harry Potter and the Sorcerer's Stone, Harry Potter and the Chamber of Secrets* and *Harry Potter and the Prisoner of Azkaban*. Under each chapter heading there will be a short synopsis of that chapter followed by a list of the relevant words, phrases and/or cultural references from that chapter, all accompanied by an explanation. Sometimes these will be brief, sometimes long—wait until you see how much information there is just to explain the word tea!

The words or concepts will be explained the first time they pop up in the J.K. Rowling novels. For instance, the word 'tosh' first appears in Chapter Four of *Harry Potter and the Sorcerer's Stone,* so that's the section in which it will be defined in this book. But what if you're reading *Chamber of Secrets* and come across a word you're not familiar with and it's not explained in that section of this guide? That's easy. At the back of this book, you'll find an alphabetical Index that will refer you to the section where the word first appears. All you have to do is flip back and find the definition. And please note, the page numbers next to each entry in this book refer to the page numbers in the Scholastic American hardback and trade paperback editions of the Harry Potter books.

I hope you enjoy reading this exploration of Harry's British world as much as I have enjoyed writing it and that you find this book fun and easy to use.

Finally, I would like to thank J.K. Rowling for giving us this incredible series of books that are filled with so much wonder, excitement and magic.

- Part One -

Harry Potter

AND THE
SORCERER'S
STONE

– CHAPTER 1 –
THE BOY WHO LIVED

CHAPTER SUMMARY:

The Dursleys are a seemingly regular English family. You'd never know—and they'd rather you didn't—that they have wizards and witches for relatives. Little do they realize that their one-year-old nephew, Harry Potter, has just witnessed the murder of his parents at the hands of the evil Lord Voldemort, and that the boy has somehow survived and defeated the mighty wizard. The orphaned Harry needs a family to raise him and the Dursleys are his closest relatives. So, one night late in October, he is delivered to the Dursley's doorstep by Albus Dumbledore, Professor McGonagall and Rubeus Hagrid. Harry is left to be raised in the Muggle (non-wizarding) world.

NUMBER 4 PRIVET DRIVE (PAGE 1)

In the very first sentence of the book, we receive our initial clue that we've entered into an alien world—and by alien, I mean British. The British often write or say the word 'number' before the actual number of a street address. That explains Number 4 Privet Drive (though it would more commonly be written as No. 4 Privet Dr.)—but what's a privet?

A privet is the most common bush or shrub used in British hedges. A neatly-trimmed privet hedge is the default perimeter of British front gardens the way a white picket fence is the default perimeter of American front yards.

GARDEN FENCES (PAGE 1)

When we say garden, we usually mean a vegetable or flower garden. The British, however, use the word 'garden' the way we use 'yard': any piece of land around a house with grass on it. Where we say front yard, they say front garden. Where we say back yard, they say back garden. To the Brits, in fact, a yard is specifically *not* a garden. To them, a yard is a paved patio, usually at the back of a terraced house (what we'd call a townhouse) in a working class (blue collar) or middle class part of town. And what we call a garden, they would usually define more specifically as a vegetable or flower garden.

When Mrs. Dursley looks over a 'garden fence' to spy on her neighbors, she'd be looking over a wooden fence (or sometimes a wire one) that surrounds or abuts her garden.

HALF PAST (PAGE 2)

It's half past eight when Mr. Dursley leaves for his office and I think that's worth noting. Not because it's the magical time when he gets to escape from his horrible family but because people rarely say eight-thirty in England. In the British world, time is told as minutes or blocks of minutes past the hour (i.e. half past, quarter past, ten past, etc.). Just watch *Mary Poppins* and you'll see what I mean.

CLOAKS (PAGE 3)

On Mr. Dursley's way to work, he sees lots of strange people wearing cloaks. Even though 'cloak' is a word we Americans use, it is somewhat rare and antiquated. We would more commonly call it a cape. But think Count Dracula more than Superman—roomy and full length with a good chance of a hood. Obviously, the cloak is a fashion must-have in the wizarding world.

FLOOR (PAGE 3)

In the building where he works, Mr. Dursley's office is on the ninth floor. Or is it? Because in the U.S., his office would be on the eighth floor. Confused? So was I. Until I found out that what we call the first floor, Brits call the ground floor. The next floor up (our second floor) is their first floor. And so on. If you ever ride in an elevator (which they call a lift) in Great Britain, you'll find this information to be extremely valuable especially when you are trying to get out of that building.

BUN (PAGE 4)
When Mr. Dursley crosses the road to buy a bun from the bakery, he's making a beeline for what we might call a sweet roll—a doughy pastry cooked with raisins and covered with icing. In this particular case, though, he ends up buying a doughnut instead. And, yes, their doughnuts are like ours, though for years their selection was pretty much limited to the glazed or jelly variety, a situation only improved by the influx of American chains like Dunkin' Donuts.

COLLECTING TIN (PAGE 4)
Over there a 'tin' is what we call a 'can.' For instance, they would buy a tin of tuna or a tin of beans. When Brits stand on a street corner raising money for charity, they carry 'collecting tins' into which other people can put their donations. Years ago, they collected money in actual cans but nowadays a collecting tin is a plastic cup with an attached handle or stem that makes it look like a bulky and unbreakable wine goblet.

Mr. Dursley assumes the cloaked 'weirdos' are wearing costumes as part of their charity-collecting efforts. Boy, is he mistaken!

GARDEN WALL (PAGE 5)
As we've learned, a garden is a yard. But a garden wall is different than a garden fence. A fence is usually wooden; a garden wall is made of stone or brick. So, when Mr. Dursley pulls into his driveway after work and sees the tabby cat (which turns out to be Professor McGonagall) sitting on his garden wall, she's perched upon a stone or brick wall in front of his house.

KENT (PAGE 6)

When Mr. Dursley watches the news, he learns that shooting stars have been spotted all over Britain including by people from a place called Kent. England is one of the countries that makes up The United Kingdom of Great Britain and Northern Ireland (see *Britain* in the index, or read further in this chapter). Where the U.S. has 50 states, England has 48 counties (which is something, given that England is smaller than many of our states!). Kent is one of those counties. It is located in the extreme southeast corner of England and lies along the English Channel (a big body of water that separates England and France).

Kent is known as the Garden of England because so much of the country's vegetables are grown there. It is also known for its vast deposits of chalk. There is a line of chalk hills which runs east to west through the middle of Kent called The North Downs. Also, on the coast of Kent, great chalk cliffs rise up in areas along the English Channel. These cliffs were romanticized in a song made famous during World War II, *The White Cliffs of Dover*—Dover being the city from which most people cross the English Channel on their way to France. And during the war, there were lots of British (and other) soldiers who did precisely that.

In the 1st century, the Romans invaded Kent (along with the rest of England). By the 5th century, the Jutes and Saxons came along and established Kent as one of the seven kingdoms of Anglo-Saxon Britain.

The beautiful gothic Canterbury Cathedral is located in the city of Canterbury in Kent. It's there that the Archbishop of Canterbury, Thomas Becket, was murdered in 1170. For years, pilgrims traveled to Becket's shrine to pay him tribute and in the 14th century Geoffrey Chaucer described these pilgrimages (with quite a bit of added flavor!) in his *Canterbury Tales*.

In *Sorcerer's Stone*, the fact that shooting stars have been seen over Kent tells us that there are wizards celebrating in this historic county east of London. But as we are about to learn, there are fireworks going on in much more far-flung places.

YORKSHIRE (PAGE 6)

In the northeast of England is the region of Yorkshire. Yorkshire used to be the largest county in England but in 1974 it was broken up into smaller counties for political reasons. On a map, you can still find the region of Yorkshire by going north (quite a bit north) from Kent.

The Yorkshire region borders the North Sea to the east and is famous for its moors—great expanses of vast, desolate and beautifully wild countryside where a flowering shrub called heather grows.

Like Kent, Yorkshire became ruled by the Romans and the Anglo-Saxons but in the 9th century, it was invaded by the Danes from Denmark. Anglo-Scandinavian culture was prevalent in Yorkshire until the Normans from the Normandy region of France took over all of England in the 11th century.

In England, people from Yorkshire are called northerners—which makes sense being that they are from the north. But just like in the U.S., people from the north and south of the the country are as different as chalk and cheese (as the Brits would say). They speak with wildly different accents (although most of us think that all English people sound vaguely the same) and often regard each other with varying degrees o f suspicion, condescension and/or disdain. That is, until they get to know each other. Because that's how prejudice works, kids. It evaporates once you make friends with the people who are different from you. (Hey, don't we learn this lesson in the Harry Potter books?!)

DUNDEE (PAGE 6)

Our last shooting star sighting comes from Dundee—a city in Britain that is not in England. Take out your map again and travel due north from the region of Yorkshire. As you move above England, you'll come to the country of Scotland. Continue along the coast of the North Sea past Edinburgh and you'll find Dundee. (If you get to Aberdeen, you've gone too far).

The town of Dundee, which dates back to the 12th century,

has a bloody history. For its first five hundred years, the people of Dundee had to defend themselves against a relentless invader—the English. Though centuries have passed, many Scots remain somewhat wary of their English neighbors to the south.

Today, Dundee is the third largest city in Scotland. Not only is it a fishing town, Dundee is where they make marmalade (the joys of which will be recounted later in this book).

The fact that wizards are celebrating as far north as Dundee leads me to conclude that in Harry Potter's Britain wizards must be everywhere!

BONFIRE NIGHT (PAGE 6)

Jim McGuffin, the weatherman, jokes that folks are observing Bonfire Night a week early. You may be thinking, what the heck is Bonfire Night? And why don't we have it here? Keep reading and all will be revealed.

Bonfire Night is celebrated every November 5th in Britain. That date is important, because it tells us when Harry is delivered to the Dursleys' doorstep. If it is a week before November 5th, Harry clearly arrives in Little Whinging sometime in late October, possibly on Halloween night itself. You might be thinking, that can't be right. There weren't any trick-or-treaters on Privet Drive that night. Well, for your information (and to my horror), although the Brits celebrate Halloween, there is no trick-or-treating there (at least there wasn't any trick-or-treating there when *Sorcerer's Stone* was written. That has changed to some degree over recent years.) I know this because when my English niece came to visit when she was little, I took her trick-or-treating for the first time. She loved it and I racked up major auntie points. But I digress.

Bonfire Night goes back to the early 17th century during the reign of the Protestant king, James I. It all started because this guy named Guy Fawkes, a Roman Catholic, plotted to blow up the Parliament building with King James I inside of it. Parliament, by the way, is somewhat like our Congress and is divided into two bodies: The House of Commons and the House of Lords. The House of Commons, like our Congress, is comprised of elected officials. The House of Lords (also called the House of Peers) are not elected at all. They are members of the peerage (see *Lords*), people who come from the British nobility and, more recently, people who are appointed, called Life Peers. Old school peerages can be passed on to descendants, life peerages cannot. (again, see *Lords*, because this stuff is confusing!)

Anyway, Guy Fawkes was upset because King James was making life pretty horrible for him and his fellow Catholics and he thought something had to be done. So, Guy and some of his mates (friends) planted about 20 barrels of gunpowder in a cellar underneath the Houses of Parliament. The conspiracy (that came to be known as the Gunpowder Plot) backfired on poor ole Guy. James I survived but Guy Fawkes was caught and put to death (drawn and quartered and burned—don't even ask). The lesson here: Violence doesn't pay, especially when you try to kill a king who already wishes you were dead.

Today, British people celebrate the death of Guy Fawkes on the aptly named Guy Fawkes Day (also called Bonfire Night) every November 5th. The classic pattern throughout the 20th century and doubtless the pattern that J.K. Rowling grew up with goes as follows: A week or so before November 5th, kids would make their *guy*—a smaller than life-size effigy of a man who represents the dead Guy F. Some kids (surely with the aid of their parents) would work very hard to make a convincing dummy. But others would simply stuff an old sweater with rags for its body and paint a face on a soccer ball for its head. Then they'd carry (or push in a baby carriage) this big doll to the nearest street corner and ask passersby for money using the time-honored cry "Penny for the Guy." Of course, with inflation, were a passing adult to actually give them a mere penny, said adult would receive a mouthful of juvenile British abuse. After several days of collecting this money, the kids would go to their local newsagent (news stand) or sweet shop (candy store) and buy as many brightly colored boxes of potentially fatal gunpowder-filled fireworks as they could afford.

On November the fifth itself, a bonfire would be built in the back garden or even in the street. The *guy* who helped them collect all this money would be rewarded for his work by being propped on top of the bonfire. The bonfire was lit, the *guy* was burned to symbolic death and the fireworks were set off in celebration.

As you can imagine, the newspapers of November 6th in the 1950s, 60s, and 70s were filled with stories and statistics about children mutilated in fireworks accidents. Consequently, just as with our Independence Day, the Guy Fawkes Day celebration has become a more publicly organized event. Now, on the evening of November 5th, people gather to watch huge firework displays. And as for the actual bonfire and the burning of the *guy*? Like Guy Fawkes himself, they're fading into history.

Bonus Question: Where have we seen the name Fawkes in *Harry Potter* and what does it have in common with the Guy Fawkes Day ritual? (For the answer, see *Fawkes*).

BRITAIN (PAGE 6)

As Mr. Dursley sits in his armchair reflecting about 'shooting stars all over Britain' (which includes Kent, Yorkshire and Dundee), he's thinking of much more than just England. We should all know this from geography class but for those of us who have forgotten, Britain consists of four countries: England, Scotland, Wales and Northern Ireland. (The rest of Ireland is not part of Britain because the Irish kicked the Brits out during the Easter Rebellion of 1916.)

Britain is technically known as the United Kingdom or the U.K.—or more precisely, The United Kingdom of Great Britain and Northern Ireland. This is the full title of the political entity, which we casually call Britain or the U.K. (or even England, much to the chagrin of the Welsh, Scottish and Irish). For the purposes of this book, I use the United Kingdom, the U.K., Great Britain and Britain almost interchangeably (even though they aren't exactly interchangeable.) But come on, people! I'm doing the best I can here! When I use the terms England, Scotland, Wales and Northern Ireland, I'm referring specifically to those countries within the United Kingdom.

TEA (PAGE 7)

Mrs. Dursley's small act of carrying two cups of tea into the living room (often called a 'lounge' by the Brits) opens the lid on a very integral part of British life—tea. Someone could write a dissertation on tea rituals and the uses of the word 'tea' in the British world (including countries in the British Commonwealth like Australia, New Zealand and South Africa). Tea is a very big deal for them. Bafflingly so. We can't possibly begin to understand how deeply rooted the tea leaf is in their culture.

When I first started going there and saw the tea thing in action, I wondered why we Americans didn't have this incredible attachment to tea, too. Then it hit me. Anybody heard of the Boston Tea Party? If George III hadn't enacted a tax on tea that resulted in a boycott of tea in the American Colonies, we would probably be just like them in the tea department. But alas, a single moment in history can change everything.

But back to Brits and their tea. There's afternoon tea, high tea, tea that's served any time, and tea that really means dinner. Let me explain...

Afternoon Tea: Afternoon tea started in England in the 19th century. The ritual is credited to Anna Maria Russell, Duchess of Bedford. Back then, the aristocrats or nobility usually ate dinner around 8pm, so Anna Maria found herself peckish (that's a Brit word for hungry) one afternoon and asked her servants to bring a pot of tea and snacks to her bedroom chamber. Hunger pangs averted, our duchess started inviting her friends to join her for afternoon snacks and tea. This became known as 'afternoon tea' or 'low tea' because ladies would sit in low armchairs sipping tea and snacking on dainty scones, cakes, finger sandwiches and the like. Afternoon tea was traditionally served around 3:30 or 4pm, sometimes followed by a promenade or walk in a local park or field.

Finger sandwiches (little wedge shaped sandwiches with the

crust cut off) are made of white bread which is spread with butter (Brits do not use mayonnaise on their sandwiches) and filled with cucumber or smoked salmon (or some other ingredient that really doesn't say sandwich to us—definitely not peanut butter and jelly!).

Scones (rhymes with johns) look like what we call biscuits—you know, the soft warm fluffy kind that grandmothers or the Pillsbury Doughboy make. But scones are denser, sweeter and to my taste less appetizing than their melt-in-your-mouth cousin. (Sidebar: what the Brits call biscuits, we call cookies.) Scones should be served slathered with butter (the real kind—which by the way is so much better in the U.K.) or covered with clotted cream. Yes, I said *clotted* cream. It's as rich, thick and artery-clogging as it sounds! Clotted cream is unlike anything we have in the U.S. Take our old-fashioned whipping cream and multiply by ten. Thicker. Heavier. Deadlier. Top with jam and you've got the perfect British scone. Afternoon tea can also include pastries and crumpets. More about crumpets later.

Oh, I almost forgot the most important part—the tea! There are all kinds of teas with different names that make no sense to us, so here's a very small sampling:

Lapsang Souchong: One of the most popular teas for tea drinkers in the U.K., Lapsang Souchong tea comes from a tea leaf grown in China. It's a smoky flavored black tea; its name translates to "the small leaf cultivar smoked by pine wood." China, by the way, is the largest tea producing country in the world.

Darjeeling Tea: Darjeeling tea is an Indian tea that actually got its start in China when Archibald Campbell (a civil surgeon in the Indian Medical Service) brought Chinese tea plants to India from Nepal in the 1840s. Mostly grown as black tea, Darjeeling tea can also come in the green, white or oolong varieties and is known for its floral aroma. The name comes from the Darjeeling District in West Bengal, India where our Scottish born, tea maverick Archie C. had a very big impact on the future of tea drinkers everywhere.

Earl Grey: Earl Grey is traditionally a black tea blend which is flavored with the oil of bergamot. A Bergamot is a type of orange grown in France and Italy. Also called "Earl Grey's Mixture," it was probably named after the British Prime Minister (1830-1834) Charles Grey, 2nd Earl Grey, after he received a diplomatic gift of bergamot flavored tea.

English Breakfast Tea: One of the most popular tea blends in the U.K. It usually is made from tea grown in Ceylon, Assam and Kenya. English Breakfast Tea is black and robust. Good to drink with breakfast or anytime. Goes great with milk and/or sugar. And it's the tea that my husband keeps in a tea tin (a metal decorative container) in our kitchen and we drink it everyday.

There are many other types of teas but this can get you started. Served in a teapot, and poured in cups resting on saucers, most Brits take milk in their tea and maybe sugar. Rarely, lemon.

Now on to high tea …

High Tea: As Americans, we often call afternoon tea 'high tea.' It's something that fancy U.S. hotels offer on Sunday afternoons and it's exactly that—fancy. But the roots of high tea are not fancy at all. High tea originated as an early dinner (say 6pm) after a full day of work by working people—who were hungry long before 8pm and didn't have the luxury of afternoon tea to tide them over. It was called high tea because it was served at the dinner table instead of at a lower table surrounded by armchairs.

Tea as Dinner: A descendant of this kind of high tea is simply using the word 'tea' to mean dinner. This is my favorite usage. I learned it from my husband who was raised in the north of England in a city named Liverpool near a street called Penny Lane. When he was growing up, they called dinner 'tea.' In this particular instance, tea has nothing to do with the drink but everything to do with the food. It's often used in blue collar or middle class households to refer to the family dinner, but not a dinner in a restaurant. An 'upper class' person in the U.K. (their term, not mine) would never refer to dinner as tea. Instead, he or she would say 'supper.'

In Chapter One of *Harry Potter and the Order of the Phoenix*, Dudley lies to his mother about having tea at his friends' houses when in actual fact, he has been roaming the streets acting like a bully. Don't be fooled into thinking that big old Dud is nibbling on finger sandwiches prepared by Piers' mother. The kind of tea that J.K. Rowling is most likely referring to here is a full-on meal—something we would never expect Dudley to pass up.

Tea that's served any time: You might have guessed by now that Brits are a bit fanatical about their tea. So it doesn't take much to surmise that in reality, they drink it at lots of different times during the day—from first thing in the morning to last thing at night. Whenever they finish an activity, you're almost sure to hear the phrase: *Who wants a nice cup of tea?* Or something to that effect. And before waiting for a response, they're off to make a pot. When in the U.K., I am constantly suffering from a tea-induced caffeine buzz. My mother-in-law would insist that that's impossible, that there's no caffeine in tea. The lesson here: never trust your mother-in-law.

Truth alert! These days, most Brits drink tea in mugs with a tea bag thrown in. The tradition of brewing tea in pots, for the most part, has fallen by the wayside for everyday use. But in my American home, my husband still makes multiple pots of tea throughout the day and I have learned there is a proper way to brew tea.

Warning to Americans: Never tell a British person that you know how to make tea. You will do it wrong and embarrass yourself and they will never let you forget it. But, for those who would like to take a stab at making proper tea for yourself, here is the procedure as I have learned it:

1. First, boil enough water to fill your teapot in a kettle. An electric kettle is best. An electric kettle sits on every British kitchen countertop.

2. Take your Brown Betty (or other traditional English teapot), pour some boiling water into it and swirl it around. This is called warming the pot.

3. Discard the water.

4. Measure out the right amount of loose tea and put it in the

teapot. No, not tea bags if you want to do it properly. Use real hon-est-to-goodness tea leaves from a jar. When using a regular-sized teapot that serves about four people, the right amount of tea would be five heaped teaspoons—one for each person and 'one for the pot.' Note that Brits hate American brands of tea and think we have no taste for it whatsoever so if you really want to do it correctly, go to a British shop and get some proper British tea. Everyday standard brands are Typhoo or PG Tips. If you don't have a British shop in your town, some of the bigger supermarkets might carry Jackson of Piccadilly or Twinings brands. (If you're using tea bags, which most people do, three bags will do in a teapot that serves four.)

5. Fill the teapot with the boiling water from the kettle and stir the pot to let the tea leaves settle.

6. Put on the lid and let it steep for five-eight minutes.

You probably think it's time to pour the tea. Alas, you are not British. At this point, most Brits pour a little bit of milk into the bottom of their cups. Never cream, only milk.

Now, finally, it's time to pour. Tip the teapot over the cup with one hand, while holding a tea strainer (which catches the loose tea leaves so they won't go in your cup) in the other and fill your perfect cup of tea. You may add a lump or two of sugar. Then stir. A cup of coffee sounds like a whole lot less trouble about now, doesn't it?

And this, for now, is my definition of tea.

Front Garden (page 7)

When Mr. Dursley looks down from his bedroom window at the cat in his front garden, he's looking down into, you guessed it, his front yard. A British front garden could be covered with grass or it might be spread with pebbles or wood chippings instead. Also, flowers or flowerbeds could be planted there. And most likely, this front garden would include a small driveway. Just like in an American front yard, the British front garden can be host to a variety of growing and non-growing things.

PAVEMENT (PAGE 9)

Professor Albus Dumbledore magically extinguishes all the street lamps on Privet Drive so that no one can see him or the catlike Professor McGonagall on the pavement. In this case, 'pavement' does not signify the paved asphalt surface on the road in front of the Dursleys' house. It means the paving stones or sidewalk alongside the street. Because in Britain, they call the sidewalk the 'pavement.'

FANCY (PAGE 9)

This word has many meanings in Britain. Like us, they use it to denote something ornate or special. But unlike us, they also use it to express a desire for something. For instance, my sister-in-law, Judith, might say, "I fancy a cup of tea." That means she'd like a cup of tea. (Everything always comes back to tea!) Also, when a boy has a crush on a girl, you might say that he 'fancies' her. And when Dumbledore tells the cat (McGonagall), "Fancy seeing you here..." he means, "Imagine seeing you here." Because 'fancy' can also mean an unusual idea or an imaginative thought.

SWEET (PAGE 10)

When Dumbledore refers to a lemon drop as a "Muggle sweet" (i.e. a candy favored by non-wizards), he uses 'sweet' as an all-purpose word that means candy. You could also call a chocolate bar or a peppermint a sweet. Note: The term 'sweetie' is used to describe candy by little children.

YOUNG SIRIUS BLACK (PAGE 14)

In the night sky, Sirius (pronounced almost like 'serious') is the name of a star that is also known as the Dog Star. As we learn later in *Harry Potter and the Prisoner of Azkaban*, this name turns out to be a very appropriate one for Mr. Black.

In *Sorcerer's Stone*, all we know about Sirius Black is that he has lent Hagrid his motorcycle to take Harry to Privet Drive. But since Hagrid refers to him as "Young Sirius Black," does this mean that Sirius is too young to own a motorcycle? Perhaps not, because to preface a name with 'Young' can mean a few different things to the British:

A. It's an endearing way for an adult to address or refer to a child.

B. It's a condescending way for an adult to address or refer to a child.

C. It's a fun and/or endearing way for grown men to address or refer to each other.

In this instance, Hagrid is making use of the last definition (C.) to describe the grown up Sirius Black.

BRISTOL (PAGE 15)

Hagrid and the baby Harry Potter fly over Bristol on their way to the Dursleys' house. Bristol is a city in England situated along the Bristol Channel on the west shore of England just south of Wales. Around the 11th century, Bristol became a settlement called Brycgstow which in Old English meant "the place at the bridge." Soon after, Bristol gained its royal charter. It became an influential shipping port and is now a popular tourist destination. But one of my favorite things about Bristol is its rich and sweet history because, back in 1795, a man with a vision named Joseph Fry patented a way of grinding cocoa beans that led to the invention of the modern day chocolate bar. So thank goodness for Bristol and Joseph Fry!

LONDON UNDERGROUND (PAGE 15)

This is the official name of the London subway system which is a network of trains that run underground throughout the capital city. Construction began on the Underground in 1866 and its initial three-mile line opened in 1890. Built in the shape of a tube that the trains run through, the London Underground was the first electric subway in the world.

Outside the Dursleys' house, Professor Dumbledore tells Professor McGonagall and Hagrid that he has a scar above his left knee "that is a perfect map of the London Underground" (that must be some scar!). In London, you see the map of the Underground everywhere and it illustrates how this fantastic subway system links the entire city. The Underground itself is relatively safe and highly popular. Mostly Londoners call it by its slang name, the Tube.

MILK BOTTLES (PAGE 17)

This is for those of you who were not born when milk used to be delivered to houses in the U.S.A. Years ago, when I was very very young, one would put empty glass milk bottles out on the front or back doorstep to be collected by the milkman who in turn delivered the new ones. In Britain, this tradition lasted longer than it did here. In fact, you can still get your milk delivered there—even though these days most people pick up the plastic gallons or the quart cartons in the supermarket just like we do.

– CHAPTER 2 –
THE VANISHING GLASS
O—O

CHAPTER SUMMARY:

Ten years have passed since Harry took up residence with the Dursleys—Uncle Vernon, Aunt Petunia and cousin Dudley. They treat Harry badly and make him sleep in the cupboard under the stairs. Harry has never been told about his wizarding heritage and thinks his parents died in a car crash. But all his life strange things have happened to Harry that make him think he is different. On Dudley's birthday at the zoo, Harry speaks to a boa constrictor in the reptile house and accidentally sets the snake free. This infuriates the Dursleys and makes Harry's life with them even more unbearable.

BACON (PAGE 19)

Bacon? Why is that a British thing, you say. We have bacon. Yes we do, but guess what? Their bacon is different from our bacon. Sure, it all comes from the same source (Wilbur) but instead of being streaked with fat and fried to crispy perfection, their bacon is meatier and softer than ours with a single strand of fat that runs along its top edge (known as the rind). Its texture is more like southern ham or Canadian bacon.

Like our bacon, the British version comes in thinly sliced rashers that are sealed in plastic. But unlike our bacon, it is cooked until done, not until crisp, like a thin piece of fried ham (that tastes really good, I might add).

But let's just say the Dursleys wake up one morning with a hankering for American-style bacon. Well, there is an option. It's called streaky bacon. Sold in supermarkets but less popular than regular British bacon, streaky bacon is very much like our own. Problem is, they don't cook it long enough. This version will certainly be a letdown to those of you who love extra crispy American bacon.

So, if one day you find yourself in England or Scotland or Wales or Northern Ireland ordering bacon, don't be surprised if it doesn't look exactly like you expected. My advice: Enjoy the difference. You can always have crispy bacon when you get back home.

CUPBOARD (PAGE 19)

When we say 'cupboard,' we mean a cabinet with shelves—like a kitchen cupboard. But the Brits also use cupboard to describe almost any kind of closet. For instance, Harry sleeps in a "cupboard under the stairs." This is a small closet situated under a staircase which has a slanted ceiling to accommodate the stairs that are right overhead. A cupboard under the stairs is a common feature in British homes. In general, cupboards are places where British people keep clothes, brooms, linen, toys and sadly, young Harry Potter.

CLASS (PAGE 20)

This one confused me for the longest time but it is actually very simple. A class is a group of 25-30 students in the same grade who go to all the same classes (courses) together. For us, it would be like going to homeroom in the morning and then staying with that same group of fellow students as you change classes throughout the entire day. This explains why Harry, Ron and Hermione have the same course schedule at Hogwarts. They are in the same class.

PARCEL (PAGE 21)

When Dudley picks up the nearest parcel to unwrap on his birthday, he is simply grabbing another birthday present. Like us, Brits use the word 'parcel' to describe something that is sent through the mail (or as they call it, the 'post') but they also use parcel to describe anything that is wrapped and which you intend to open—like a Christmas or birthday present. So while a gift is covered with wrapping paper, it is referred to as a present *or* a parcel. Once it's been unwrapped, it's just called a present.

ADVENTURE PARKS (PAGE 22)

Adventure parks are places where Brits visit to go on roller coasters and other rides. To us, these would be big amusement parks like Six Flags or even Disneyland (minus the princesses and overgrown mice).

MAD (PAGE 22)

"Mad Miss Figg" is not an angry old woman but a crazy or insane one. Just think of the Mad Hatter from *Alice in Wonderland*. He certainly didn't get that name because he was filled with wrath. He's just bonkers. Although we might say 'mad' to denote craziness *or* anger, the Brits would not. They would only say mad to mean angry if they get it from American TV (which they get lots of over there) because this usage does not come naturally to them. There is an exception: If someone were to really lose his temper, you could say he 'went mad.'

MAJORCA (PAGE 23)

Pronounced Ma-york-a (with the stress on the second syllable). Majorca is the largest of the Balearic Islands, which rest in the Mediterranean Sea off the coast of Spain. It's where many British people go on holiday (vacation) and make a nuisance of themselves with such habits as wearing t-shirts with the charming message *Speak English or Die*. (For those Brits who may stumble upon this book, please send hate mail to my English husband whom I credit entirely for that last part of this definition).

HAVE A GO (PAGE 23)

When Harry hopes to "have a go" on Dudley's computer, he

hopes to have a 'try' or a 'turn' on it. In other words, he desires a chance to use it. In addition, someone can want to 'have a go' at someone else, meaning they want to fight or attack them, physically or verbally. What do you bet that Harry would sometimes like to have a go at Dudley?

MUMMY (PAGE 23)

No, this is not an ancient undead Egyptian wrapped in bandages who crashes through your French doors to try to kill you. This in fact means Mother or Mommy. Shortened, our 'Mom' is their 'Mum.'

HEADMISTRESS (PAGE 25)

A headmistress is a female school principal. A headmaster is a male principal. A school in the U.K. has either one or the other just like we have only one principal at each of our schools.

VAN (PAGE 26)

When the Dursleys buy ice cream at the entrance of the zoo, they are not purchasing their scrumptious delights from some hippie in a van. That's just what the Brits call an ice cream truck—an ice cream van.

KNICKERBOCKER GLORY (PAGE 26)

Hasn't Dudley had enough ice cream for the day?! Apparently not if he's having a knickerbocker glory. This is an old fashioned dessert found nowadays mostly in touristy or seaside cafes. Served in a tall parfait glass with a long spoon, a knickerbocker glory consists of many layers of yummy and/or interesting elements, depending on your taste.

Starting from the bottom of the glass with the first or bottom layer, the ingredients are as follows:

1. Ice cream: two scoops of vanilla.

2. Jell-O: (which they call jelly) in lime, strawberry, raspberry or cherry flavor.

3. Cream: the kind you pour on.

4. Fruit: the canned or tinned type. Could be peaches, pears, pineapple, gooseberries, fruit cocktail or a mixture of any or all of the above.

5. If there is enough room in the glass—though how would that be possible?!—repeat layers again beginning with the ice cream.

6. Top the concoction with whipped cream and a glazed cherry. And that, my friends, is a knickerbocker glory!

SWEET TEA (PAGE 29)

I include this for readers in the southern U.S. When the contrite zoo director serves Aunt Petunia sweet tea, he's giving her a cup of hot tea with some sugar added, not the iced, syrupy variety I grew up on in Georgia. Remember, the British drink their tea with milk and/or sugar, rarely with lemon and even more rarely with ice.

– CHAPTER 3 –
THE LETTERS FROM NO ONE

CHAPTER SUMMARY:

Summer vacation starts and Harry gets ready to go to the local high school. But then the letters start arriving. More and more of them—all addressed to Harry. The Dursleys try to hide the letters from Harry and flee the city in an attempt to keep the letters from finding him. But it's no use. The letters keep coming. Panicked, Uncle Vernon takes a boat and rows his family and Harry out to a little shack on a rocky island in the sea. There, as the clock strikes midnight, and it becomes Harry's eleventh birthday, a visitor arrives at the door.

SUMMER HOLIDAYS (PAGE 31)

Summer vacation. For Harry, these particular summer holidays take place during the break between the end of his Muggle school year and the beginning of his time at Hogwarts. In the U.K., they rarely use the word vacation at all, even when talking about going on a trip. That is called a holiday, too. For instance, many Brits go on holiday to Majorca (see *Majorca*).

LOT (PAGE 31)

Dudley is the "biggest and stupidest of the lot." That means he is the biggest and stupidest of the group. (Like we didn't know that already). 'The lot' (or 'you lot' or 'their lot', etc.) is a term that can be used to mean any kind of gaggle, group or gang.

SECRETARY SCHOOL (PAGE 31)

High School. Except British students, called pupils (they don't really get called 'students' until they are at university) start secondary school (also called senior school, very rarely called high school) at age eleven. Secondary school lasts for seven years but it is only mandatory for the first five of those years. At the end of the fifth year, at the age of 16, students take their GCSE O Levels. This stands for General Certificate of Secondary Education Ordinary Level and are usually referred to as 'O Levels.' These O Levels consist of a week or two of exams in eight or more subjects. If a student passes six of these exams, he or she would receive or 'get' six O levels. At this point said student would acquire an O Level Certificate (like our high school diploma) and could enter the job market.

However, if this same pupil desires further education with an eye to going to university (they rarely say college unless referring to a college within a university or a vocational school), he or she must pass a certain number of O Level exams (determined by his or her school) to be accepted into the '6th Form.' That is what they collectively call the last two years of high school, the years individually being called the 'Lower 6th' and the 'Upper 6th.'

At the end of the 6th Form, at age eighteen, students take more exams—the GCSE A Levels or General Certificate of Secondary Education Advanced Level. The results of the A Levels are very important when it comes to being accepted to a university, in the way that our general grades and SAT scores determine our university viability here.

There is another difference between our school systems that I think is worth noting. What we call private schools, the English refer to as public schools. And their state schools (or as we would say, our public schools) are called either grammar or comprehensive schools. Truly, it boggles the mind.

Note: this definition is based on my husband's school experience which would have been similar to J.K. Rowling's school experience, which informs the Hogwarts experience in the Harry Potter books.

LONDON (PAGE 32)

The largest city in England and the capital of the United Kingdom (which as we know is also referred to as Great Britain or the U.K.) Founded by the Romans, London was originally called Londinium. It is a beautiful old city which rests along the River Thames (pronounced Tems). Like many rivers in England, the word 'river' precedes the actual name of the waterway.

It was in London that William Shakespeare wrote his great plays and Sir Christopher Wren built St. Paul's Cathedral. It was there that the kings and queens of England lived and ruled and where the Houses of Parliament were built. However, for all its beauty, this glorious city has seen much destruction—from the Great Fire of London in 1666 to German bombing raids during World War II.

In London, you find Buckingham Palace (where the Queen lives), the Tower of London (where the Crown Jewels live) and an old church called Westminster Abbey (where lots of famous dead people live).

UNIFORM (PAGE 32)

There is nothing unusual about Dudley and his mum going to London to purchase his school uniform. That's because the majority of British students wear uniforms to school. Since Dudley is planning to attend Smelting (an English public school, meaning it would be a private school to us), his uniform would be more formal than the type Harry would be required to wear at the local secondary school.

But in general, there are some basic elements that make up most any school uniform. These include:

1) Gray or black pants for boys. Sometimes skirts for girls.

2) White shirt.

3) A jumper in a school color. (A jumper is what we call a sweater).

4) A blazer, also in a school color, with the school's crest on one of the breast pockets.

5) A tie. In secondary school, both boys and girls are required to be equally uncomfortable by wearing these. Like the jumpers and blazers, school ties would reflect the school's colors.

But as we are about to see, Dudley's duds take the basic school uniform to a rather bizarre level.

TAILCOATS (PAGE 32)

Dudley's uniform for Smeltings is very formal if he must wear tailcoats. Think tuxedo jacket with tails. Prince William wore tailcoats when he was at school at Eton (the exclusive public school in Windsor).

KNICKERBOCKERS (PAGE 32)

These are loose-fitting pants that gather just below the knees. In years past, knickerbockers were worn primarily by boys, men playing sports, and bicyclists. Also, women would wear them as undergarments (called bloomers). The word 'knickerbocker' comes from Diedrich Knickerbocker, the pseudonymous name under which Washington Irving wrote *A History of New York From the Beginning of the World to the End of the Dutch Dynasty* in 1809. George Cruikshank illustrated the book and his drawn Dutchmen wore these kinds of pants. A knickerbocker also became the slang term for a New Yorker, hence the basketball team, the New York Knicks.

Nowadays, we call knickerbockers, 'knickers.' But if you say 'knickers' to a Brit, they'll think you're talking about underwear. There's an expression here: *Don't get your panties in a wad.* Well, in England, it's: *Don't get your knickers in a twist.*

BOATERS (PAGE 32)

Tailcoat, knickerbockers and now a boater! Dudley's got some outfit going here. A boater is a men's old-fashioned summer straw hat that was worn originally when, funnily enough, boating. It was stylish years ago in the U.S. as well as the U.K., but today? And on the modern, round head of Dudley Dursley? Ridiculous is the word that comes to mind.

ISLE OF WIGHT (PAGE 34)

The first mention of Aunt Marge comes with her postcard from the Isle of Wight, which happens to arrive the same day Harry gets his first letter. The Isle of Wight (pronounced white) is an island off southern England in the English Channel. It's a big vacation spot that boasts some of the best weather in all the British Isles. It is also home to a whole lot of chalk. A ridge made entirely of the white stuff crosses the island and makes up the thickest chalk in the entire United Kingdom. (Think about that next time you're at the blackboard.)

Also, 'Wight' is an old Anglo-Saxon word that means 'man.' But wait! There's another British island called the Isle of Man (located off the coast of England in the Irish Sea). So technically they've got two islands with the same name. And who said geography wasn't interesting?

LITTLE WHINGING (PAGE 34)

This is the village where the Dursleys live and where Harry receives his first letter from Hogwarts. Although Little Whinging might be the name of a real town (because heaven knows they have some strange town names over there), I suspect this is one of J.K. Rowling's jokes. Because in England, to whinge (rhymes with hinge) means to whine. And there is no greater whining family in all of England than the Dursleys.

SURREY (PAGE 34)

It's revealing to learn that Little Whinging is set in Surrey—a county in the southern part of England, southwest of London along the River Thames. This means the Dursleys live close enough to London to drive or take the train in, but they do not live within the city limits of London itself.

The landscape of Surrey is varied and beautiful, partly because of two ridges that cross the county from east to west, one of them being The North Downs which also traverses Kent.

The history of Surrey goes something like the history of Kent and the rest of England. The Romans invaded, followed by Anglo-Saxons, then the Normans. By the time of Henry VIII (the guy who liked to behead his wives), the hilly forests of Surrey became a hunting ground for the rich and famous and Henry himself built a hunting lodge there. But as the population grew, so did an immense suburban network of railway lines that originated from London. In the 19th century, this network became the largest of its type in the world.

Today, Surrey is part of the Stockbroker Belt, one of the areas around London from which many people commute to the 'City' (what people call the financial section of London, like our Wall Street).

PARCHMENT (PAGE 34)

Before there was paper, there was parchment. Parchment was a finely prepared leather product made from goat or sheepskin, which was developed into a writing material around 190 B.C.E. Vellum (a term often used interchangeably with parchment) was made from calfskin.

The development of parchment is significant. The books we read today are direct descendants of the early codices (bound books) made possible by the invention of parchment. But more about that in a minute. First, let us step back in time so we can gain a broader perspective of this thing called parchment.

The first so-called books were made of clay tablets. People in Mesopotamia (around the area of Iraq today) would squash out a piece of clay, scribble on it and let it dry in the sun. Next, came the much improved papyrus (pronounced pa-pie-rus with the stress on the second syllable), which is more like the paper we use today. The Egyptians (clever folks, the Egyptians) harvested the papyrus plant that grew in the Nile Valley and processed it into sheets, which would be pasted together to create rolls—or scrolls. These rolls became the dominant writing material in Egypt and elsewhere. In fact, the great works of ancient Greece and Rome were written on papyrus. Papyrus—from which our word 'paper' descends—reigned as the writing medium of choice for quite a long time.

Until a great book collecting rivalry changed everything.

Book Collector Number One came from Egypt. Ptolemy V

had many scribes (people who copied manuscripts by hand in the centuries before printing was invented), and they would reproduce the words of great books onto rolls and rolls of papyrus for his great library in Alexandria.

Meanwhile, Book Collector Number Two—Eumenes II of Pergamum—was following the same routine for his library in Greece.

Threatened by this competing library, Ptolemy V did something rather devious. He placed an embargo on the papyrus made in Egypt that prevented it from being imported into Greece.

This put Eumenes II in a quandary. What was he to do? There were books to be copied but nothing to copy them on. But, as necessity is the mother of invention, he found a way. Thus, the invention of parchment. At least, that's how the story goes. And since the word parchment in Greek and Latin means 'stuff from Pergamum' many people believe this version of the story of parchment to be true.

Parchment was produced by washing, stretching, scraping and smoothing animal hide into an ideal writing surface. Okay, I know the animal skin part sounds disgusting but you must keep in mind that the invention of parchment was a big deal. A very big deal. It was strong and flexible and, because of this, people could write on the front *and* the back of it. Like papyrus, parchment was often produced in rolls—very much like the rolled variety that Harry, Ron and Hermione regularly use for their course work (although Hogwarts hopefully employs parchment paper rather than the original animal hide kind). But more notably, parchment made way for a revolution in bookmaking that would eventually leave the papyrus roll in the dry Egyptian dust. Its flexibility and durability allowed for the development of the codex—the book. Now are you starting to see why parchment was so important?

By the 4th century C.E., parchment became the dominant manuscript material used in Britain and the rest of Europe. During the Dark Ages (after the fall of the Roman Empire), it allowed for the production of great illuminated books—beautiful tomes that were hand copied by monks throughout the continent (most notably in Ireland). These books became pieces of art that also served the purpose of spreading the Gospel of Christianity.

Charlemagne (born 742), who went from being the king of the Franks to the Holy Roman Emperor, was instrumental in saving great secular written works. His dedication to collecting and copying ancient texts preserved much of the classical literature that had survived into the 8th century. And it was because these works were copied onto the lasting materials of parchment and vellum that we have them still today.

At this point you might be wondering: when did we get paper? Well, wonder no longer. Because while parchment was being utilized in the west, paper was invented in the east. The Chinese (clever folks, the Chinese) developed paper in the 2nd century C.E. But it took a thousand years for papermakers to make their way to Spain and Sicily. And then three hundred more for them to wend their way to Germany. Right on time for the invention of the Guttenberg printing press. History is just full of happy coincidences.

But even though paper had arrived, the tradition of bookmaking with parchment greatly influenced the newfangled technology of printing. That is because printers copied the model of the parchment book—pages bound together, etc. But have you ever wondered why our modern books are taller than they are wide? Again, this comes from the parchment model. You see, in order to get the most out of each animal hide, parchment pages were cut in this manner. Even though paper could have been cut to any size, the standard had already been set and printers conformed to it.

Today, we cut down trees to make books, but for over a thousand years, people sacrificed poor defenseless animals. A high price to pay, especially if you were a sheep or a goat. Luckily for animals everywhere, today's parchment is usually made of high quality paper. Perhaps the story of parchment will inspire a new and improved writing material that will save another one of our defenseless friends—the tree. Or maybe that's already happened with the e-book.

COAT OF ARMS (PAGE 34)

When Harry receives his first letter from Hogwarts, the envelope is sealed with purple wax which bears a coat of arms (wax was used to seal envelopes in the days before the lick-and-stick variety). A coat of arms, also called a shield of arms, is a graphic design, like a logo. First used in Europe in the 12th century to establish identity in battle, coats of arms were later designed for families, universities, churches and other organizations as well. The basic design usually consists of a shield containing four fields or sections, which are decorated with symbols and colors to represent and identify a particular group. The coat of arms on the back of Harry's letter is that of Hogwarts. Its symbols are the animals that represent each school house (the lion, the eagle, the badger and the snake) and the large letter H identifies the school itself.

WHELK (PAGE 35)

When I read that Aunt Marge ate a "funny whelk," a whole host of silly sea dwellers came to mind. Was she dining on a laughing lobster or a peculiar puffer fish? No, she just ate a 'funny' or spoiled large sea snail. Sounds delicious (argh)!

PORRIDGE (PAGE 35)

The kind of food we read about in fairy tales and Charles Dickens' novels. But really, it's just oatmeal—a soft cereal boiled in milk or water. For us, unlike oatmeal, the word porridge conjures up visions of other times and other worlds. For Harry and the Dursleys though, porridge is just a simple something you have for breakfast.

POSTMAN (PAGE 39)

What we call the mailman. We used to call him the postman too, at least according to anyone old enough to remember the Marvelettes' 1961 hit *Please Mister Postman* (or the 1963 cover version by four mop-topped Brits who in their day were almost as famous as Harry Potter).

POST (PAGE 41)

Although the editors at Scholastic have carefully substituted the word 'mail' for 'post' throughout this chapter in the American Edition, a 'post' does slip through (lucky for me). Uncle Vernon announces "No post on Sundays." As you can guess, that simply means no mail on Sundays. Just keep in mind, wherever we use the word 'mail,' they use the word 'post.'

MARMALADE (PAGE 41)

Usually one does not spread marmalade on a newspaper, even though a flustered Uncle Vernon does. Mostly marmalade is spread on toast or scones. And sure, we can buy it in stores here but again, marmalade a much bigger deal over there. Traditionally, marmalade is a jam-like preserve made from oranges, containing rind and pulp. What makes it different from regular jam is its bittersweet taste. In the U.K., you can also buy lemon or lime marmalade, just the thought of which makes my face contort.

TINNED TOMATOES ON TOAST (PAGE 42)

Say that ten times fast! Tinned tomatoes on toast are what we would call canned tomatoes on toast. Believe it or not, this is a common quick lunch or snack item in the U.K. You heat the canned tomatoes up in a pan and then pour them over a couple of pieces of toast. What will they think of next?

COKEWORTH (PAGE 42)

The letters find Harry at the Railview Hotel in Cokeworth. The name of this hotel and town richly illustrate the Dursleys' location. Picture a grimy coal town full of coal yards (or coke yards). Industrial, gray, unwelcoming. Then, imagine the Railview Hotel—old and rundown, situated next to a railroad track where trains used to load up with coal for their long journeys. Definitely not a hot vacation spot.

EH? (PAGE 44)

Usually used at the end of sentences for extra emphasis, the word 'eh' also turns that sentence into a question (often a rhetorical one). It's one of those words that has to do with inflection. In the shack on the sea, Uncle Vernon uses it ironically. But throughout the books, it's utilized in a variety of ways—from emphasizing a dark warning to highlighting a humorous reality. Hagrid and Ron seem to employ it best, eh?

− CHAPTER 4 −
THE KEEPER OF THE KEYS

CHAPTER SUMMARY:

Hagrid arrives at the shack with a birthday cake for Harry along with the true story of Harry's past which the Dursleys have kept from him all these years. Harry learns that he is a wizard and finally receives his acceptance letter from Hogwarts School of Witchcraft and Wizardry.

HAGRID'S ACCENT (PAGE 47)

Although introduced in Chapter One, it is in this chapter that we first experience the full glory of Rubeus Hagrid's accent and slang. Perhaps he's not a well-spoken man, but he is certainly full of heart and *so* much fun to read.

In the movies, Robbie Coltraine (a man from Scotland) plays Hagrid and brings his accent to life for us. He speaks in the rural voice of someone from Somerset or Cornwall in the southwest of England. Parodoxically, Maggie Smith (a woman from England) lilts in a Scottish accent in her portrayal of Professor McGonagall.

US (PAGE 47)

When Hagrid says "Couldn't make us a cup o' tea?" he is not asking that cups be prepared for everyone. This is an example of where 'us' means 'me.' Hagrid could have also said (like my husband often does) "Gis a cup of tea" which is an ancient elision of "Give us a cup of tea." Both mean "Give *me* a cup of tea." Trust me, this Brit-speak takes a little getting used to.

BUDGE UP (PAGE 47)

Scoot over. That's what Hagrid tells Dudley to do as he approaches him on the sofa in the shack. And if I were Dudley, I would budge up fast!

GREAT (PAGE 47)

Whereas we mostly use great to denote importance or talent, Hagrid uses it to denote size, i.e. "yeh great lump" or "yeh great prune" ('yeh' is just how Hagrid says 'you') Here great means huge or gigantic. In other words, it means Dudley Dursley.

SUMMAT (PAGE 47)

Something (in Hagrid's accent).

MESELF (PAGE 48)

Myself. Used mostly by everyday, blue-collar people, especially in the north of England. Not likely to come out of the mouth of Queen Elizabeth or Professor Dumbledore.

MIND (PAGE 48)

Short for 'mind you.' Hagrid uses it idiomatically here. For us, it can translate to: if you don't mind, bear in mind, or be aware.

KETTLE (PAGE 48)

As we now know, it is very important to make tea the right way, so much so that Hagrid carries around his own copper kettle. Remember, you boil water in a kettle before pouring it into a teapot.

TEAPOT (PAGE 48)

That into which you pour the boiling water. A teapot is a pot with a handle, a spout and a little lid used for brewing and pouring tea (see *tea*). As noted earlier, the brown betty is the most traditional English teapot but there are all kinds—from the very plain to the extremely ornate. Mostly they are made of pottery but a formal tea service could come with a silver teapot.

PUDDIN' (PAGE 49)

When Hagrid refers to Dudley as "yer great puddin' of a son," he's being a bit mean but also a bit funny ('yer' is how Hagrid pronounces 'your'). 'Pudding' means a type of dessert. (I'll be more specific later). So literally, Hagrid is calling Dudley a big fat dessert. But as he uses it figuratively here, he means that Dudley is a big and useless boy.

MARKS (PAGE 49)

Marks are what we call grades. Like grades, marks are based on a 100 percent possible score and are denoted as letters (A-F). My husband tells me the grading system in England is more stringent than it is here. But seeing that he never went to an American school, do you think I should believe him?

BOIL YER HEADS (PAGE 50)

Idiomatic expression that roughly means 'get stuffed' or 'get lost.' Usually said by someone who is cross, annoyed or fed up. Like Hagrid is with the Dursleys.

THUMPIN' (PAGE 51)

Thumpin' is a word that would be used by people of the rural south of England, like Hagrid. When he states that Harry would be a "thumpin' good" wizard, Hagrid just means he would be a darn good one.

MUM (PAGE 51)

Mom. In England, 'Mummy' is the infantile diminutive of 'Mum.'

THE SEA (PAGE 51)

Brits don't go to the ocean, they go to the sea. Just look at a map and you'll see why. The countries of the U.K. are surrounded by seas: the North Sea, the Irish Sea, the Celtic Sea (plus the English Channel).

HEADMASTER (PAGE 51)

A headmaster is a male principal of a school so it follows that Albus Dumbledore is the Headmaster of Hogwarts. However, he is referred to as Professor Dumbledore, not Headmaster Dumbledore. Replace their word headmaster with our word principal and you will understand why. For instance, I called my high school principal Mr. Moses—not Principal Moses. But I would refer to him as the principal of my high school. It is the same with Professor Dumbledore who is the headmaster of Hogwarts. No offense to Mr. Moses but if I had had a choice between him and Professor Dumbledore...

MERLIN (PAGE 51)

Professor Dumbledore belongs to the Order of Merlin, a fictitious group of wizards. Merlin is part of the legend of King Arthur that goes back to the Middle Ages in Britain. It is fabled that Merlin was a great wizard who served as an advisor to King Arthur in Camelot, an idyllic place thought by many to have been located in the southwest of England, in Cornwall.

In literature, Merlin became the prophet of the Holy Grail. Then he became a movie star. Check out *Excalibur, The Sword in the Stone, Camelot* or even *Monty Python and the Holy Grail* and you'll see what I mean.

TERM (PAGE 51)

A term is what we call a quarter or a semester in the school year. In Britain, there are three terms to a regular school year. Here we learn that Hogwart's fall term starts on September 1.

DEPUTY HEADMISTRESS (PAGE 51)

Assistant female principal. If Professor McGonagall were a man, she would be a deputy headmaster. Either way, doesn't it sound nicer than assistant principal?

GORGONS (PAGE 52)

When Hagrid exclaims, "Gallopin' Gorgons," I don't think he really means galloping mythological creatures with snakes in their hair—but then again, you never know with Hagrid! If you've studied Greek mythology, you'll remember there were three Gorgons, sisters named Stheno, Euryale and Medusa, and they all had the power to turn whoever looked at them to stone. The mortal Gorgon, Medusa, was killed by Perseus. He used his shield as a mirror so that he could look at her without being turned to rock. Then he cut off her head. Ouch.

QUILL (PAGE 52)

Used everywhere before the steel-tipped pen was invented, a quill was made of a stiff feather with a hollow stem, the end of which was sharpened into a nib. You would dip the quill periodically into an ink well to refill the stem with ink as you wrote.

Before the quill, people wrote with reed pens or brushes. By the 6th century, the quill became the dominant writing instrument and it stayed that way until the mid-19th century. So when you think about people writing on parchment, now you know what they were writing with.

The best and strongest quills were taken from live birds, mostly from geese (sounds painful to me). The favored feathers came from swans and ravens. As we learn in *Harry Potter*, the quill seems to be the preferred writing implement in the wizarding world.

RUBBISH (PAGE 53)

A very popular English word that means nonsense—which is precisely what Uncle Vernon thinks of wizardry. But 'rubbish' also literally means 'trash.' For instance, they don't have trash cans, they have rubbish bins.

GARGOYLES (PAGE 54)

"Gulpin' gargoyles." Another Hagridism. We don't have a lot of gargoyles on buildings in this country but they are loaded with them in Europe. Originally, in Roman architectural structures, gargoyles were carved lions that functioned as waterspouts to drain water from the gutters of buildings. In the Gothic Period, the gargoyle was most often carved as a grotesque bird or a squatting beast. So if you're in London or Paris (or even New York) and walk past a real old building, look up. You just might see one.

BLIMEY (PAGE 54)

An exclamatory word that in present day Britain is very common and inoffensive. Blimey is an abbreviated (and sanitized) version of 'Cor Blimey,' an old curse that goes back centuries and is itself a shortening of 'God blind me' or 'God blight me.' Again, it's one of those words that Hagrid would use much more readily than say, Professor McGonagall.

HEAD BOY (PAGE 55)

The chief boy prefect (see *prefect*). My English husband equates the head boy (in fact, all prefects) to 'trusties'—those brown-nosing prisoners who help out the guards in a prison. But Hagrid might regard a head boy as a respected leader of the student body. Harry's father was one. And Percy Weasley will be one. Two different personalities, both head boys. Maybe this tells us our definition should fall somewhere between these two extremes.

HEAD GIRL (PAGE 55)

The chief girl prefect. Harry's mother was one.

HALLOWEEN (PAGE 55)

It's here that Hagrid confirms what we suspected earlier. That

Harry was first delivered to the Dursley's doorstep on Halloween night.

The British celebrate Halloween but as I said before, it wasn't until recently that they embraced the tradition of trick-or-treating. When my husband was growing up (oh so many years ago), they would have Halloween parties where kids would play games. The standard ones were duck apple and bob apple. Think you know which is which? Because duck apple is what we call bobbing for apples. You know, a bunch of apples in a tub of water that you try and grab with your mouth. The other game, bob apple, is where you attempt to grasp an apple with your teeth as it hangs from a string.

After all that incredibly unsanitary germ swapping, candles would be lit and children would gather round to tell ghost stories. The climax of the evening would take place when a father would jump out to scare them wearing a monster mask. (Here we learn that British fathers aren't so different from American ones).

Tosh (page 56)
Another term that means nonsense or something ridiculous. Uncle Vernon calls Hagrid's story about Harry's past a "load of old tosh." He could have just as easily called it a load of old rubbish.

Sticky End (page 56)
To end badly or to come to an unpleasant conclusion. This is what Uncle Vernon expected would happen to Harry's parents—and sadly he was right.

Codswallop (page 57)
It is no lie that the Brits have a lot of slang words that mean roughly the same thing and codswallop is one of these words. Like 'rubbish' or 'tosh,' it means nonsense. Although the origin of codswallop is not certain, it is thought to have been derived from Hiram Codd's marble-stopped mineral water bottles, which he patented in 1875. Codd's Wallop became a term that beer drinkers would

derisively call mineral water or other less than potent drinks. (Wallop is archaic slang for beer). Over the years its specific meaning has been watered down for general consumption.

CLOUTED (PAGE 57)
Harry has "spent his life being clouted by Dudley." It doesn't take a rocket scientist to figure this one out. Clouted means hit, smacked or punched—all things which Dudley Dursley does so well.

FOOTBALL (PAGE 57)
When you think of Dudley kicking Harry "around like a football," are you envisioning an American pigskin? If so, think again. Because football in the United Kingdom (and the rest of the world) is what we call soccer. And their football is a soccer ball. Soccer is by far the most popular sport in Britain.

RIGHT (PAGE 58)
If Harry is 'right' famous, he is simply very famous. But if 'right' is used to *preface* a sentence (like on p. 71 of *Sorcerer's Stone*), its meaning is more like 'Okay,' 'All right' or 'Listen up.'

ME (PAGE 59)
Interchangeable with 'my.' For instance, you could say "Where's me shirt?" or "I'm ready for me cup of tea." Me is used this way especially in the north of England or Ireland. My husband says it a lot.

KEEN (PAGE 59)
Although keen can mean many things, one of the primary usages over there is one we seldom employ. When Hagrid says he was 'keen' to be the one to come and find Harry, he means he was eager.

THIRD YEAR (PAGE 59)
Hagrid confesses that he was expelled from Hogwarts in his third year. There are seven grades in the British secondary or high

school. But instead of grades, they are referred to as years. A third year student (age 13-14) would be in his or her third grade of secondary school, equivalent to our 8th grade.

GAMEKEEPER (PAGE 59)

Literally, this means keeper of the game. There are still some gamekeepers on private aristocratic estates in Britain whose job it is to care for the game (usually wild birds like pheasant and grouse) until the master of the manor is ready to hunt said bird. Hunt is a euphemism for shooting a poor defenseless bird in cold blood after it's released from its cage, for the sport of it.

KIP (PAGE 60)

One of my all time favorite British slang words! To 'kip' is to sleep. It can be used as a verb as Hagrid does ("You can kip under that") or as a noun ("I just had the best kip"). Fun and childlike—simply put, kip is a perfect word.

DORMICE (PAGE 60)

The plural for dormouse. A dormouse is a small European rodent, which is similar to a squirrel. I don't know about you but if there were dormice in Hagrid's pockets, I wouldn't be kipping under that coat.

CHAPTER 5

DIAGON ALLEY

CHAPTER SUMMARY:

Hagrid and Harry ride the Underground to London to a magical pub called The Leaky Cauldron where they meet the Hogwarts Defense Against the Dark Arts teacher, Professor Quirrell. Then, at Diagon Alley, the wizards' secret street of stores and shops, Harry collects some money (from the fortune his parents has left him) from Gringotts Bank and accompanies Hagrid to Vault 713 to pick up a secret package. While shopping for school supplies, Harry has his first encounter with Draco Malfoy and receives a gift from Hagrid, Hedwig the owl. Last stop—Ollivanders Magic Wand Shop where the wand that chooses Harry turns out to be the 'brother' wand of the one that picked Lord Voldemort.

HUMBUGS (PAGE 62)

The humbug is an old fashioned hard candy. Peppermint humbugs are usually swirled or striped in colors of red and white or black and white. But instead of the wheel shaped peppermints to which we are accustomed, the British variety is oblong and rounded. There are also golden humbugs that are shaped like little 3-D triangles or pyramids and taste of toffee or mint.

When I visited Stratford-Upon-Avon (Shakespeare's birthplace) with my husband and in-laws, we went into an old-time candy store (or, in Brit-speak, sweetshop) where there were jars and jars of different types of humbugs. I learned that the word 'humbug' was first used as a slang term for a practical joke or a hoax. It wasn't until the 19th century that it came to describe the hard candy that we're talking about here.

In Charles Dickens' *A Christmas Carol*, Ebenezer Scrooge employs it in yet another way. When he exclaims "Bah, Humbug!", he is not yelling for Bob Cratchit to fetch him a peppermint. Scrooge is using 'humbug' to mean hypocritical nonsense. (How many words can there be for nonsense?!)

TEABAGS (PAGE 62)
I know I taught you earlier to make tea in a teapot with loose tea. But nowadays most Brits use teabags for everyday use. Why? Because it's easier! Here's how:
Put a teabag in mug.
Pour in steaming water from kettle.
Let steep for a few minutes.
Remove teabag with spoon.
Add milk.
Sorted. (that's Brit-speak for 'done')

FETCHIN' (PAGE 63)
Or fetch. All right, we all know what fetch means—you throw the stick and the dog brings it back. But in the U.K., 'fetch' is used for much more than dog games. Hagrid has come to fetch Harry but Brits can fetch almost anything. It means to go somewhere to get something or someone and then bring back that thing or person. Often you fetch something that's been left behind. In the case of Harry, he's been left behind for ten long years!

HIRED (PAGE 63)
Harry and Hagrid go back to the mainland in the boat that Uncle Vernon hired. This sounds strange because over here, we hire people, not objects. But in Britain, they do both. You don't rent a boat or a car there. You hire it. But like us, they would rent a house or an apartment—the latter of which they refer to as a 'flat.'

MINISTRY (PAGE 64)

In Britain, they call government departments 'ministries.' Where we would say the Defense Department, they would say the Ministry of Defense, etc. As far as I know, there is no actual Ministry of Magic in England...yet.

MINISTER (PAGE 64)

This is the person who runs the Ministry. In the British world, ministers head up government departments. And the minister that presides over them all is the prime minister. The prime minister is somewhat like our president but isn't individually elected. He or she is the leader of the political party that is currently in power. Their most famous prime minister was Winston Churchill who saw his country through World War II.

BUNGLER (PAGE 65)

This is what Hagrid disparagingly calls Cornelius Fudge, the Minister of Magic. A bungler botches things up—something that Hagrid is sure Fudge does on a consistent basis.

CRIKEY (PAGE 65)

Like blimey, 'crikey' is one of those strange but wonderful words that I was first introduced to with regularity by my sister-in-law, Judith. It's an inoffensive exclamation of surprise or shock. It can also mean something as benign as 'Gee!' Here Hagrid could say, "Gee, I'd like a dragon." (But aren't we glad he doesn't.) Remember how we learned that 'Cor Blimey' was a watered-down version of 'God Blind me!'? Well, most etymologists agree that Crikey originated as some sort of less-offensive euphemism for 'Christ!', even if they can't agree on what the original phrase was.

FIRST YEAR (PAGE 66)

In his list of school supplies, Harry is informed that first years are not permitted to bring broomsticks to school. Harry is about to become a first year student at Hogwarts (age 11-12), which is equivalent to our 6th grade, the grade when most American kids are beginning middle school. But in Britain, their secondary or high school starts at this earlier age.

Note that on the spine of each of the Harry Potter books, there is a year number that corresponds to Harry's grade level during that book.

HERBS (PAGE 66)

The British pronounce the 'h' in the word 'herb' and think it is peculiar that we do not. Their argument: It's got an 'h' in it!

TICKET BARRIER (PAGE 67)

When Hagrid gets "stuck in the ticket barrier on the Underground," it means the big guy got trapped in a turnstile on the way into the subway. What a sight that must have been.

CINEMAS (PAGE 68)

When Hagrid and Harry pass a cinema in London, that means they're passing a movie theater. Even though we use movie theater and cinema interchangeably, Brits do not. A movie theater is only called a cinema there. The word 'theater' is reserved for live performances and is spelled 'theatre.' Also, instead of saying to friends, "Let's go to the movies," a British bloke (see *bloke*) would more likely offer, "Let's go to the pictures."

PUB (PAGE 68)

Short for public house—but nobody calls a pub a public house anymore. A pub is a place where people meet in a village, town or city to share a drink and a conversation. It can also be a place to play darts, skittles (an ancient European ancestor to ten-pin bowling), or watch the football (soccer) on TV. It's a cozy community bar of sorts which can be the public focal point of a village. Pubs have their origins in Roman taverns which sprung up almost two thousand years ago, and evolved into charming old watering holes. They are part of British communities where people meet and drink (something at which Brits truly excel) and sometimes eat (in the case of the pub restaurant). Common pub names that you might encounter are The Pig and Whistle, The Rose and Crown, The Coach and Horses, The Crown and Anchor and The King's Head. Most large American cities are home to at least one British-style pub—sometimes owned by some good-humored expatriate from the British Isles.

VAMPIRES (PAGE 70)

One who sucks and drinks human blood. The most famous vampire, Dracula, was imagined by an Irishman named Bram Stoker back in 1897. *Dracula* tells the story of the eponymous vampire from Transylvania who, in his coffin, stowed away on a ship called the *Demeter* and travelled to England. Where bad stuff happened. (Some pretty bad stuff happened on the *Demeter*, too.)

MUST GET ON (PAGE 70)

For us, this translates to 'must get going' or 'must get a move on.' It's what Hagrid says to the others at The Leaky Cauldron to expedite his and Harry's departure. After all, Diagon Alley is waiting.

BLOKE (PAGE 70)

A chap (see *chap*), a fella, a guy. 'Bloke' is an informal word that is used commonly in Britain to refer to a man or an older boy. In this case, the bloke is Professor Quirrell.

BLACK FOREST (PAGE 71)

The Black Forest sounds like a made-up forest for wizards, but it's not. It's a real region in southwest Germany—a large mountainous forest range covered with fir trees which supposedly make it so dense that it's black. According to Hagrid, the Black Forest is inhabited with vampires and hags. Luckily for me, I missed the vampires and hags when I was there.

HAG (PAGE 71)

From 'Haegtesse,' an Old English (aka Anglo-Saxon) word for witch. In European and British literature and legend, a hag is an ugly old woman who engages in witchcraft, or a fairy or spirit who takes on the form and appearance of such. Both versions sound like the kind of chick you don't want to bump into, but—like witches—they've probably gotten a bad rap over the centuries from scaredy-cat men.

APOTHECARY (PAGE 71)

Harry and Hagrid pass by an Apothecary in Diagon Alley. This is what we would call a pharmacy or a drugstore. In the U.K., this kind of store is usually called a chemist or a chemist's shop.

POUND (PAGE 76)

The pound is the primary unit of currency in the United Kingdom—like we have the dollar, the Europeans have the euro and the Japanese have the yen, etc. The value of the pound can vary. I've seen it soar to almost twice the value of a dollar, and I've seen it dip closer to one dollar. The exchange rate is affected by world events and other economic factors.

Except for the one-pound and two-pound coins, pounds are issued in notes or bills that carry the picture of the current monarch on them. Five pound and ten pound notes are now made of polymer, not paper, with the twenty pound and fifty pound notes to follow.

Like here, a pound is also a measurement of weight. But whereas my mother-in-law used to buy a pound of sugar, these days our English niece would more likely purchase sugar measured in kilograms or grams. When weighing yourself in Britain, pounds are translated into stones. A stone is equal to 14 pounds. So a Brit who weighs 181 pounds would say he weighs 12 stone and 13 pounds.

HOUSE (PAGE 77)

A school house. We all know the houses at Hogwarts— Gryffindor, Ravenclaw, Hufflepuff and Slytherin—but did you know that this comes out of a real tradition of school houses in British public (private) schools? Like at Hogwarts, Muggle school houses are represented by different colors. Their main purpose is to create teams for sporting competitions within a school—the most popular of which are football and cricket.

As I said before, the Brits call soccer football. And when you think about it, doesn't that really make sense? Last time I checked, soccer was still played with your feet—unlike American football, which is played with all the extremities. Over there, a soccer ball is called a football and soccer players are football players (or, more often, footballers).

Cricket, another popular British sport, is somewhat similar (stress on the *somewhat*) to our baseball. It's played with a pitcher (which they call a 'bowler') and batters (called 'batsmen') and there are innings and runs. But that's where the similarities end! It's taken me years to teach my English husband how American baseball works but I still haven't a clue when it comes to cricket.

At Hogwarts, there's no football or cricket. Because at this wizarding school, it's all about Quidditch.

I SAY (PAGE 78)

The snobbish boy in the Robe Shop (who we discover later is the incredibly snobbish Draco Malfoy) says "I say, look at that man" when he sees the enormous Hagrid outside the shop window. 'I say' is simply a meaningless expostulation to add urgency to what follows. It's like us using the word 'hey' before a sentence but in a more posh (upper class) way. Growing up, it seemed to me that every Englishman in every old movie said "I say" at the beginning of every sentence. It was quite a common expression in the first half of the 20th century and even these days, every now and then a Hugh Grant or a Colin Firth might let one slip.

BRILLIANT (PAGE 78)

When Harry tells Malfoy that Hagrid is brilliant, he doesn't mean that he's sparkly or smart (although brilliant means those things in the U.K., too). In this case, he means Hagrid is great or fantastic. This is a very popular usage.

DUFFERS (PAGE 80)
Useless, no good losers. Bet the Hufflepuffs wouldn't take kindly to Hagrid calling them duffers. Would you?

PAVING STONES (PAGE 80)
Remember when we learned that the sidewalk is called the pavement in England (see *pavement*). Well, paving stones are the concrete or stone sections that make up the sidewalk. Harry sees books as large as paving stones in Flourish and Blotts. Those must be some enormous books!

DEAD (PAGE 81)
Not just an old stiff, 'dead' is also an adjective which means very or extremely. For instance, when Hagrid tells Harry that having an owl is "dead useful," he means that having an owl is very useful. Dead can be used in a positive or negative way. Something can be dead good or dead bad, practically 'dead' anything.

PHOENIX (PAGE 84)
The phoenix is a beautiful, mythological Arabian bird that lives for a number of years before burning itself to ash. Then out of those ashes, it is reborn into a new bird with a new life.

In ancient Egypt, the phoenix represented immortality and was associated with the Egyptian god of the sun, Ra. Later, in Europe, the phoenix became the symbol of the alchemist. The study of alchemy led to the emergence of medical chemistry and the establishment of the chemist's shop (or pharmacy). Like the alchemists before them, these chemists adopted the phoenix as their 'logo' and the image of the bird adorned their signs.

In Mr. Ollivander's store, Harry buys a wand that contains a feather of a phoenix. In *Harry Potter and the Chamber of Secrets*, we meet Professor Dumbledore's bird, Fawkes, who is a phoenix.

BOWED (PAGE 85)
In fancy stores in days gone by, sales clerks would literally bow to their customers as they escorted them out of their shops. In Diagon Alley however, Mr. Ollivander is probably not literally bowing to Harry and Hagrid. Most likely, he is simply giving them a polite nod as he sees them to the door.

PADDINGTON STATION (PAGE 86)
This is the railway station where Hagrid takes Harry to start his woeful trip back to the Dursleys. The station is named after the London district in which it resides. Like many mainline (overground) stations in London, there is a tube (subway) station of the same name beneath it. Paddington is located at the far northwest corner of the Underground system.

Another famous character from English children's literature is the marmalade-loving (see *marmalade*) Paddington Bear who was named after Paddington Station when he was found there by the Brown family in the first Paddington book (*A Bear Called Paddington*, 1958, by Michael Bond). A bronze statue of Paddington Bear wearing his floppy hat resides in Paddington Station today. The fictional character is such a beloved fixture of British culture that British tunnellers handed a soft, stuffed Paddington through to French tunnellers when the two sides broke through to each other when digging the Channel Tunnel in 1994. Also called the Chunnel, the Channel Tunnel is the train tunnel linking England and France under the English Channel.

KING'S CROSS (PAGE 87)
King's Cross is a major train station in London where you can catch overground trains to places throughout the country. It's a huge, magnificent, neo-Gothic monstrosity—probably somewhat like

Hogwarts itself. Located in central London, a little to the north, it also houses the King's Cross Underground Station.

– CHAPTER 6 –
THE JOURNEY FROM PLATFORM NINE AND THREE-QUARTERS
$9\frac{3}{4}$

CHAPTER SUMMARY:

Uncle Vernon drops Harry off at King's Cross Station where he first meets the Weasley family who show him how to get onto Platform Nine and Three-Quarters. Once on the Hogwarts Express, Ron and Harry get to know each other and Harry meets Ron's rat, Scabbers. When a fast-talking girl bursts into the compartment, Harry and Ron have their first encounter with Hermione Granger. The mood sours when Draco Malfoy and his thugs, Crabbe and Goyle, show up, and Harry and Draco become adversaries. Finally, they arrive at Hogwarts where Hagrid takes the first year students across the lake by boat to the castle.

PLATFORM (PAGE 89)

Platform Nine and Three-Quarters would be called Track Nine and Three-Quarters in the U.S. A track is the railroad equivalent of a gate in an airport. It tells you where to catch your train in the terminal. Now, next to the train track itself is a concrete surface on which you stand to wait for your train, and we do call that surface a platform (like the Brits do). But we name the place after the track that the train runs on, while they name it after the platform you stand on to catch the train.

BARKING, HOWLING MAD (PAGE 90)

Sounds like something we'd call a rabid dog but then again, we're not British. The adjectives barking and howling are often linked with the word 'mad' (remember mad means crazy there). When you're 'barking, howling mad,' you are essentially really, really crazy—which is what Uncle Vernon thinks of all wizarding people.

RUDDY (PAGE 90)

Literally, ruddy means red but it's used more idiomatically in the case of Dudley's "ruddy tail." Here, ruddy is a more polite version of the British expletive 'bloody'—a great swear word. Both words are used with regularity in Britain but whereas ruddy means something as mild as 'darn,' bloody has a stronger meaning—so don't be caught saying it around any British grown ups!

GUARD (PAGE 91)

This would not be the guard who watches over prisoners at the railway station. A guard is an all-purpose railway attendant who directs passengers to trains. You would find a guard at the booth on the platform where he or she could tell you, for example, if the train you are waiting for is running on time. Also, it's a guard's job to wave a flag to indicate to the conductor that the train ready to leave the station.

TICKET INSPECTOR (PAGE 91)

A ticket inspector inspects your ticket as you enter the platform or track. And then another inspector (this one we would call a conductor) checks your ticket when the train is en route.

TROLLEY (PAGE 93)

A cart. When you just can't carry your big heavy bag (or trunk in Harry's case) any longer, you throw it on a cart (or trolley) and roll it through the terminal. You also see these carts at baggage claim areas in airports.

CARRIAGES (PAGE 94)

What we call train cars, the English call carriages. Doesn't that sound wonderfully old fashioned? As if magical horses were going to speed the Hogwarts Express through English countryside.

GO ON (PAGE 94)
Where we would say 'come on' in an attempt to persuade someone to do something, they would say 'go on.' The kids on the train are really saying, "Come on, Lee, let us have a look at what's in the box."

OY (PAGE 94)
'Oy' gets yelled a lot by British kids like George Weasley, usually to get someone's attention. Where they would say 'Oy!' we would say 'Hey!' (Are you starting to think that their slang words are more fun than our ones?!)

GEROFF (PAGE 95)
Phonetically, this is how Ron pronounces 'get off.' And most assuredly, he's saying it in an exaggerated way due to the embarrassment he is enduring at the hands of his dear old Mum.

ICKLE (PAGE 95)
English baby-talk for 'little.' Poor Ron.

SOMEFINK (PAGE 95)
English baby-talk for 'something.' Poor, poor Ron.

BADGE (PAGE 96)
The silver badge on Percy's chest is what we would more likely call a pin—unless Percy is a sheriff and as far as I know, there are no sheriffs at Hogwarts. But no doubt, if there were, Percy would want to be one.

PREFECT (PAGE 96)
Like we have patrols in elementary school, the English have prefects in high school. Teacher's helpers (or teacher's pets), prefects are

a select group of students from the upper grades who take on student leadership responsibilities and perform duties for teachers such as taking the roll. (In the U.K., by the way, taking the roll is called 'doing the register.') 'Prefect' comes from the Latin word 'Praefectus' which in its earliest form (very B.C.E.) meant the person who looked after things for the consuls (big wigs) when they were out of the city. What do you bet that even ancient Rome had to put up with a few Percys?

LOADS (PAGE 97)

Sure, it's easy to understand what this means—lots or many. But you can't ignore the fact that Harry and his friends use the word 'loads' loads.

SANDWICHES (PAGE 101)

Even though people have probably eaten bread and meat together as long as there have been, well, bread and meat, it wasn't until 1762 that the thing we call a sandwich got its name. After the 4th Earl of Sandwich, John Montagu, spent 24 hours at a gaming table eating only sliced meat and bread so he could keep on playing, people began to call this culinary combination the sandwich. But the sandwich wasn't the only thing to gain its name from the Earl. In 1778, the explorer Captain James Cook named a group of islands in the Pacific after him. Today, the Sandwich Islands are known to us as Hawaii.

On the Hogwarts Express, Ron pulls out a bag of sandwiches that were made by his mum. These sandwiches would be different from the kind my mother would make because in Britain they spread butter on their sandwiches, not mayonnaise. I thought this very strange at first but it's really quite delicious. Particularly in the north of England, this kind of butter sandwich is often referred to as a 'butty.' A butty can be almost anything that is surrounded by two pieces of buttered bread. You can have a bacon butty, a cheese butty, a jam butty or even a chip butty—which is a bunch of French fries wrapped in bread and butter and which is, let me assure you, every bit as delicious as you might imagine it to be.

MARS BARS (PAGE 101)

Harry wants to buy a Mars Bar on the train but can't because they've only got wizarding candies on the cart. Big deal, you might say? Well, it *is* a big deal because—and you might want to sit down for this one—what they call Mars bars in the U.K are what we would call Milky Way bars. And what we call Mars bars are Milky Ways over there. The company that makes them would doubtless claim there are all kinds of sociological or economic reasons why this is so but I think it's just a ploy to confuse the poor unsuspecting American traveler.

CAULDRON CAKES (PAGE 101)

The kind of cake that Harry buys from the woman on the train is probably what we would call a cupcake. But what makes it a *cauldron cake*? Only a witch or wizard would know for sure.

PUMPKIN PASTY (PAGE 101)

Again, a pumpkin pasty is something that's been conjured up in the wizarding world. But a regular English pasty (pronounced pass-tee, with the stress on the first syllable) is a baked pastry usually filled with meat and vegetables. The most common is called a Cornish pasty.

NICOLAS FLAMEL (PAGE 103)

Nicolas Flamel was a real live alchemist who lived in France and died in 1418. Alchemists were precursors of modern scientists and one of their major aims was to discover how to turn lead into gold. It was purported that the thing that would allow them to do this was called a 'philosopher's stone.' Whether Flamel was successful in making gold all those years ago is unknown—although he did become a very wealthy man. Hmmm...

However, according to J.K. Rowling, Flamel never died and now lives in England where he is the only known possessor of the sorcerer's stone (or philosopher's stone). You might be interested to know that the English Edition of *Harry Potter and the Sorcerer's Stone* is actually entitled *Harry Potter and the Philosopher's Stone.* Guess the publisher thought that title wouldn't fly in the U.S. Do you think they were right?

TENPIN BOWLING (PAGE 103)

Our kind of bowling. Ten pins, long lanes, dorky shoes. But why the tenpin distinction? In Britain and throughout Europe, the term bowling is reserved for a much older traditional game called bowls or lawn bowls. Often played on the back lawns of pubs, bowls is an outdoor game where you roll a ball (or bowl) across the grass toward a jack (a smaller stationary ball). Whoever rolls his ball closest to the jack wins. Haven't they ever heard of marbles?

MORGANA (PAGE 103)

In Celtic mythology, she's also called Morgan Le Fay and was the sorceress sister of King Arthur. It was Morgana who opened the eyes of Arthur to the infidelities of his wife, Queen Guinevere, with the famous knight of the Round Table, Sir Lancelot. In *Harry Potter*, she is one of the many magical people represented on collectable cards in the Chocolate Frog series.

CIRCE (PAGE 103)

Another card from the Chocolate Frog series about another sorceress. This one comes from Greek mythology—stories and legends from the ancient Greeks about their gods and heroes. The oldest known works of Greek literature are *The Iliad* and *The Odyssey* (9th and 8th century B.C.E.), which are attributed to the Greek poet, Homer. Greek Mythology has had a significant impact on World literature (which of course includes British literature).

The myth of Circe comes from *The Odyssey*, Homer's epic poem that describes the wanderings of Odysseus as he tried to make his way home from the Trojan War. One of the many stops along his voyage included the island of Aeaea (okay, try to pronounce that!) where the sorceress Circe lived. Circe used her powers to turn Odysseus' shipmates to swine. Through the aid of the Greek god Hermes, Odysseus was able to escape this porky fate and he persuaded the sorceress to change his crew members back into their human forms.

Druidess Cliodna (page 103)

Also a Chocolate Frog card, Cliodna is known from Irish mythology as a goddess of beauty and of the sea. Druids held honorable positions in Celtic British society where they acted as teachers, priests and judges. (The Celts were the peoples who inhabited the British Isles before the Anglo-Saxons came.) In pre-Christian Britain, the pagan Druids held their rites in the woods and performed human sacrifices. They also believed in the immortality of the soul. After Christianity came to Ireland, the Druids no longer served as priests but continued to act as judges as well as historians and poets.

Tripe (page 104)

Although some people claim to love it, I can only define tripe this way—disgusting! For those with strong constitutions, read on. Tripe is made from a part of the stomach of an ox or cow. Yum. I don't know how it's prepared and I don't want to know. And I certainly don't want to bite into a tripe-flavored Berti Bott's Every Flavor Bean!

Curry (page 104)

As well as being a flavor in Berti Bott's Every Flavor Beans, curry is a delicious food dish from India. Made from various Indian spices, curry is a piquant sauce that adds amazing flavor to meats and vegetables.

Did you know that Indian restaurants are as popular as Chinese restaurants in the U.K.? And Chinese restaurants there (like here) are very popular. There is an Indian restaurant in almost every English town, no matter how small.

England's relationship with India and its food goes back centuries.

It is a history of commerce and conquest that grew into full-blown British domination during the Victorian era (that means during the reign of Queen Victoria, 1837-1901). Queen Victoria was the second longest ruling monarch Great Britain has ever had (the longest ruling monarch being the modern day Queen Elizabeth II). She was also crowned Empress of India in 1876. But eventually the British Empire lost its grip on India and by the time of Elizabeth II, India had gained its independence and kicked out the British for good. Since then, the Indians have used their cuisine to conquer what is left of the British Empire.

EVER (PAGE 105)

As in 'ever such' and 'ever so'—phrases Hermione uses to stress her surprise and pleasure at being accepted at Hogwarts. Used in this way, 'ever' emphasizes whatever word follows it. It can sound ever so annoying when coming out of the mouth of a know-it-all eleven year old.

HERMIONE (PAGE 106)

When I first read *Harry Potter and the Sorcerer's Stone*, I wasn't exactly sure how to pronounce Hermione's name. Now, everyone knows how to pronounce it (Her-my-a-knee, with the stress on the second syllable)—that is, unless you've been living under a rock for the past twenty years. Hermione is an old fashioned name popular in Victorian England. Your grandparents would probably remember Hermione Gingold, a famous English actress who appeared in movies like *Gigi* and *The Music Man*. Or Hermione Baddeley, another English actress who played one of the Banks' maids in *Mary Poppins*. But let's face it—for you and me, there's really only one Hermione!

SORT (PAGE 108)

When Draco Malfoy implies that the Weasley family is the "wrong sort," it sets into motion the enmity that will color the relationship between Malfoy and Harry from this day forward. In this context, we would more likely use the words 'wrong type' or 'wrong kind.' But any way you slice it, Malfoy's words paint him as an elitist bigot, which gives us the right to find pleasure every time he is outsmarted, embarrassed or defeated by Harry Potter.

ALL RIGHT THERE? (PAGE 111)

This is Hagrid's way of saying hello to Harry when he arrives at Hogwarts. "All right there?" or "All right?" are normal all-purpose greetings that used to literally mean "Are you all right?" Nowadays, this is used rhetorically when greeting someone, like we say "How are you?" In *Chamber of Secrets*, Colin Creevy almost always says "All right?" when addressing Harry. All he's really saying is "Hey Harry, how's it going?"

CASTLE (PAGE 111)

If you've ever read a fairy tale or watched a Disney movie, you know what a castle is. But there's much more to the history of the castle than being the birthplace of Prince Charming.

Developed in the 9th century in Europe, castles were medieval strongholds for the protection of the kings and lords who owned the lands all around them. On the outside, great walls with towers and turrets protected the castle. Beyond the walls, a moat (or surrounding body of water) offered an additional line of defense. The only way to cross this moat and enter the castle was by way of a drawbridge that could be raised and lowered at will. If you didn't want someone to come inside your castle, you didn't lower the bridge.

Inside a castle were features like an open-air courtyard, a great hall, living quarters, a chapel and a keep. The keep was a strong internal enclosure that served as a place into which troops could withdraw when the other defenses of the castle had failed. It also offered a line of escape from oncoming invaders.

During the 15th and 16th centuries when firearm usage in warfare escalated, the castle defense started showing holes. The medieval castle was gradually tossed aside for more modern military fortifications.

Today, there are medieval castles all over Britain. I visited Warwick Castle in the Midlands of England and got to appreciate castle architecture first hand (and I highly recommend it!). I discovered that nowadays drawbridges are always lowered—for a fee. And that the only invaders in this day and age are tourists like me.

– Chapter 7 –
The Sorting Hat

Chapter Summary:
After Harry, Ron and Hermione are sorted into Gryffindor House, they enjoy the start-of-term banquet with the other Gryffindors in the Great Hall. Dumbledore greets all the students but warns them not to trespass into the right hand side of the third floor corridor during the school year. After dinner, Harry receives a wicked look from Professor Snape that makes the scar on his forehead burn. Later, it's lights out in the Gryffindor dormitory, and a bad dream for Harry.

Smarten (page 114)

When Professor McGonagall tells the first years to "smarten themselves up" while they're waiting for the Sorting Ceremony to begin, she's not telling them to quickly gain some intelligence (although that might not be a bad idea for a few of them). Instead, she wants them to attend to their appearances and spruce themselves up for the occasion. Of course, Harry reaches straight for his hair in a futile attempt to smooth it down.

Monk (page 115)

Although a ghostly-looking monk flies over the first years, monks are usually living men who reject society for ascetic religious lives devoted to God. The development of Christian monastic institutions started in Egypt but over the years spread into Russia and Europe.

During the 6th and 7th centuries, monasteries were established in England and Ireland. It was in the scriptoria (or writing rooms) of these monasteries in the British Isles (most notably Ireland) that something wonderful occurred.

After the fall of the Roman Empire, Europe sank into a period called the Dark Ages or the Early Middle Ages (approx. 400-800 C.E.). During this time, Europe became known collectively as Christendom and acted as one enormous church-state. But without the unifying influence of the Romans, quality of life, scholarship, culture and art went into serious decline. But as Europe was descending into this dark period, Ireland was about to enter into its Golden Age—which was made possible by the monks.

In the 5th century, St. Patrick (and others) brought Christianity to Ireland. As the Irish converted to the Christian faith, they too caught the fever of conversion. Not only did they establish monasteries throughout Ireland and in Europe, they also created an amazing influential instrument for spreading the Word. It was called the 'illuminated manuscript.' These were beautiful codices or books containing the Gospels and other Christian works. The monks copied these works onto sheets of vellum and/or parchment that were then bound into great leather books. Not only did they copy all the words (by hand!), they decorated these books with elaborate and beautiful designs meant to honor their sacred contents.

Art and beauty flourished during the so-called Dark Ages through these illuminated manuscripts. The Book of Kells is one of the most famous and finest of its examples and was once known as "the chief relic of the Western world."

FRIAR (PAGE 115)

Friar comes from the Latin word 'frater' that means brother. Like monks, friars belong to religious orders but unlike monks (who usually seclude themselves from the world), friars often live as members of a community, doing charitable works and relying on charitable contributions for their livelihoods.

The founding fathers of the Roman Catholic mendicant (which literally means begging) orders were St. Francis of Assisi who established the Franciscan Order in 1210 and St. Dominic who founded the Dominicans in 1216, though eight other mendicant orders were to follow. The members of these orders, called friars, were required to live simply with few material possessions. Many friars acted as priests who relied on the charity of their congregations to get by.

The most famous friar is Friar Tuck who comes from the legend of Robin Hood, one of the earliest heroes of the English people. Like our Harry, Robin Hood was exiled from his natural place in the world and had to gather a special group of friends around him to fight against an evil lord. Friar Tuck was one of Robin's merry men. He was also his chaplain.

RUFF (PAGE 115)
The ghost talking to the Fat Friar wears a ruff which tells us that he must have been alive during the 16th or 17th centuries when ruffs were all the rage. Ruffs are high, starched and frilled collars that wrap all the way around the neck. Terribly uncomfortable and dead old fashioned.

BOWLERS (PAGE 117)
Unlike the Sorting hat, a bowler is a hard felt hat with a rounded crown. It's what we call a derby. In Hollywood, the Brown Derby restaurant sported a huge bowler hat over the top of its eatery (before its unfortunate demise). The first bowler hat was crafted in 1850 and its name either comes from the surname of its felt supplier or its designer. Nobody knows for sure. What I do know is that the bowler is a pretty cool hat that practically nobody wears anymore.

In A FLAP (PAGE 118)
When birds get frightened, they flap and flutter away. So when you're in a flap, you're in a state of being overly anxious or excited.

GOING ON (PAGE 118)

Brits say this all the time, especially my husband when he's tired of hearing me talk about the same thing for too long. At the Sorting Ceremony, Ron tells Harry that Fred had been "going on" about them having to fight a troll. But you can 'go on' about almost anything. It's when you talk on and on about something, sometimes to the point of irritation. In the case of Fred, that wouldn't take long.

HIGH TABLE (PAGE 122)

The staff table located at the top end of the Great Hall where Dumbledore, all the professors, and Hagrid sit. It's also where Harry gets his first glimpse of the dreaded Professor Severus Snape.

YORKSHIRE PUDDING (PAGE 123)

Doesn't this sound like some nice, creamy sweet dessert? Well, surprise! It's not. Yorkshire pudding is a savory soufflé that is served with roast beef for Sunday dinners (which take place on Sunday afternoons in the U.K.). Traditionally roasted or baked in the meat juice, Yorkshire pudding is made from a batter mixture somewhat similar to pancake or waffle batter, but the texture and taste are quite different. They are cupcake shaped and when cooked, Yorkshire puddings dip in on themselves so that their edges are taller than their middles, similar to soufflés. Like biscuits or rolls, Yorkshire pudding is often used to soak up gravy. We don't have anything like it and that's a shame because Yorkshire pudding is good—really good. When in the U.K., I recommend you eat loads of them!

SIR (PAGE 124)

Like kids here, a student over there would call his professor "sir" (I hope) but there is another distinctly British usage for this word. 'Sir' is used as a title of honor that prefixes a knight's name, as in that of the Gryffindor ghost, Sir Nicholas de Mimsy-Porpington (aka Nearly Headless Nick).

Its origins go back to the Latin 'senix' (meaning old man) which evolved in England into the word 'sire.' Sir is a shortening of sire and has been used for centuries as the formal title for a knight. Originally, a knighthood could only be bestowed on someone who had performed great military service for the country, but for quite some time people who have served the United Kingdom well in other ways have also been knighted. Sir Paul McCartney and Sir Elton John are two modern day examples, both musicians. Incidentally, you would never call them Sir McCartney or Sir John. When addressing someone with the title 'sir,' you always say it in combination with the person's first name, not his last, i.e., Sir Paul or Sir Elton. I hear Americans get this wrong all the time and it makes Brits silently cringe. In the case of the Gryffindor ghost, we would call him Sir Nicholas even though the kids at Hogwarts have a more unpleasant name for him.

CHAT (PAGE 124)

During the Great Depression in this country, Franklin Roosevelt would broadcast 'fireside chats' to the nation. But it's not until rather recently (maybe since the Harry Potter books came out) that 'chat,' meaning an easy or familiar conversation, has fallen into regular usage here. There are some British meanings that we haven't adopted yet though. For instance, they call a talk show, a 'chat show' and when a boy flirts with a girl, it can be said that 'he's chatting her up.'

BEHEAD (PAGE 124)

Since Nearly Headless Nick is nearly headless, he could have met his death through the ancient capital punishment of beheading which means to cut off one's head with a sword or an axe. Sadly, in Nick's case, someone didn't quite complete the job. In France, they chopped off heads by using a device called the guillotine.

Thought a noble way to die by the Greeks and Romans, beheading came to England with the Norman king William the Conqueror in the 11th century. It was a death reserved primarily for people of high stature who did something wrong or were accused of doing something wrong. The most famous woman to lose her head in England was

Anne Boleyn, second wife of Henry VIII, and mother of the future Queen Elizabeth I. The last official beheading in England occurred in 1747 and after that, hanging became the execution of choice.

Today, the United Kingdom (along with most other European countries) do not put criminals to death. Capital punishment was abolished there in 1965.

BARON (PAGE 124)

The Bloody Baron is the blood-covered ghost of Slytherin house. Baron was an old French word that (along with beheading) came with William the Conqueror to England in 1066. First, it applied to the vassal or servant of a nobleman or the king. But later, the title of baron moved up in the world and became one of the five orders of the Peerage, part of the British aristocracy (for more—much more—about the peerage and barons, see *Lords* in the *Chamber of Secrets* section).

TREACLE TARTS (PAGE 125)

Ah...desserts. At this feast in the Great Hall, there are some desserts we recognize and some we do not. Treacle tarts are somewhat like pecan pie, without the pecans, and just the goo. Treacle is the syrup that makes the goo. It is similar to molasses. And since these are tarts, they're baked into single serving morsels.

JAM DOUGHNUTS (PAGE 125)

Jelly doughnuts. What we call 'jelly,' they call 'jam.' (Jelly, in England, is what we call Jell-O or gelatin). Brits simply love jam. They eat more toast and jam over there than you can possibly imagine.

TRIFLE (PAGE 125)

An elaborate dessert made for special occasions. As explained to me by my sister-in-law, a proper trifle is a concoction of cake, custard, alcohol and fruit. The ingredients, which are layered into a bowl, include the following:

- Sponge cake or sponge fingers (lady fingers)
- Raspberry jam
- Ratafia Biscuits (plain cookies they call digestives)
- Sweet sherry
- Orange Liqueur
- Raspberries
- Custard
- Powdered sugar

You bake the trifle in a bowl and then spoon this moist dessert into individual servings. That's what I call a lot of work for a mere 'pudding.'

BLACKPOOL PIER (PAGE 125)

When Neville says his Great Uncle Algie (short for Algernon) pushed him off the Blackpool pier, that means he launched the poor kid right into the Irish Sea. I couldn't help but feel sorry for Neville when he told this story because I have been to Blackpool pier and it seemed like the coldest place on earth (and that was in October). But even in the cold, Blackpool is great. It's a city in the north of England that could be called the Coney Island of Britain with its seaside roller coasters and rides. Blackpool is also known for its Illuminations (the lights that line the boardwalk through the Fall) and its magnificent Tower (a very tall building where you can look out over the city or take a dance in its world famous ballroom).

TROT (PAGE 128)

Dumbledore sends the students to bed with the phrase "off you trot." He could have also said "off you pop." Both are common phrases for our "off you go."

COATS OF ARMOR (PAGE 129)

Also called suits of armor. You've all seen them in scary movies set in far away castles (like Hogwarts), or in cartoons where they chase the likes of Shaggy and Scooby Doo. But in real life, coats of armor were donned by medieval knights for protection in battle. Nowadays, they just seem to decorate old castles.

HANGINGS (PAGE 130)

These are the curtains that surround the boys' four poster beds in the Gryffindor dormitory. When pulled closed, they provide privacy for whatever an eleven-year-old boy needs privacy for.

– CHAPTER 8 –
THE POTIONS MASTER

CHAPTER SUMMARY:
Harry and the other first year students start their classes. Potions Class is a nightmare for Harry when it becomes obvious that Professor Snape has it in for him. At Hagrid's hut, he expresses his concerns about Snape but when he spots a newspaper clipping on Hagrid's table, all thoughts of Snape evaporate. The article tells about a break-in at Gringotts Bank, which occurred on the very day Harry and Hagrid had been there. Harry comes to believe that the burglars were after Hagrid's secret package from Vault 713.

CONK (PAGE 132)
It's pretty easy to guess that your conk is your nose. Peeves likes to grab them to irritate first year students.

DOUBLE POTIONS (PAGE 135)
Double Potions sounds like what it is. Two back-to-back school periods with the same professor teaching the same course. Like here, British schools have class periods throughout the day. But because they are required to take more subjects during a quarter than we are, class schedules vary from day to day during the week in order to fit them all in (the weekly schedule stays the same). So, on Monday, you might take a single physics class but on Wednesday, the same physics class might be scheduled over two periods. This Wednesday

class would be referred to as Double Physics. My husband says that double classes were nightmares if you hated the subject and/or the teacher. So surely, Double Potions is a nightmare for Harry.

DUNDERHEAD (PAGE 137)
A stupid person—or according to Snape, most of his students. What a way to start the school year.

CHEEK (PAGE 138)
Harry's "cheek" gets a point taken away from Gryffindor by Snape. But this kind of cheek has nothing to do with the red rosy side of Harry's face. Instead, it pertains to what Harry said and how he said it. To have 'cheek' or to be 'cheeky' means to be insolent, disrespectful, impertinent or presumptuous. But it doesn't always have a bad connotation, especially when that insolence is communicated in a charming, mischievous or funny way. As with so many words, it all depends on the person and the situation. In the case of Snape and Harry, it becomes crystal clear that Harry's 'cheek' will forever be unappreciated in Potions class.

BOARHOUND (PAGE 140)
Hagrid's dog Fang is a boarhound. Like an Irish Wolfhound, boarhounds are hunting dogs. Their specialty was the wild boar which was once hunted extensively in England and across Europe.

ROCK CAKES (PAGE 140)
Sort of like scones but harder. Especially when baked by Hagrid.

GIT (PAGE 141)
Throughout the books, we learn that this is one of Ron's favorite words. 'Git' is a dialect pronunciation of the word 'get' which in old-time farming circles (or the Bible) was used to mean offspring. The baby lamb would be the 'get' of the mama sheep, for example. But over time, Brits came to use it as a derogative term to describe a

person who was a jerk or a pig or a swine or Professor Snape. Git is the kind of rude word that kids find funny coming out of the mouth of adults—as Harry and Ron do when Hagrid calls Filch one.

Tea Cozy (page 141)

A woolen wrap for a teapot that keeps the tea warm. The tea cozy fits snuggly around the pot except where it has holes for the spout and the handle. We have a tea cozy with the design of the Union Jack (the flag of the U.K.) that fits over our teapot completely, no holes at all.

Cutting (page 141)

This is an item, perhaps an article, that is cut out from a newspaper, here from the *Daily Prophet*. We call it a clipping. The British could call such an article a clipping as well but they often refer to it as a cutting.

31 July (page 141)

No, this is not some strange way the Daily Prophet prints dates for the wizarding word, it's how Muggles do it there, too! When writing a date in Britain (and in the rest of Europe), the day precedes the month. As you can see, it's not so hard to figure out when they spell the month out, but when they don't, be prepared to feel like a right dunderhead. For instance, what do you think when you see 4/6/18? That's April, 6, 2018. Right? WRONG! In the U.K., that's June 4, 2018. It throws me every time.

- CHAPTER 9 -
THE MIDNIGHT DUEL
○-○

CHAPTER SUMMARY:
During their first flying lesson, Harry's amazing performance in the air prompts Professor McGonagall to enlist Harry into the Gryffindor House Quidditch team in the position of Seeker. But the incident sparks Malfoy to challenge Harry to a midnight duel in the Hogwarts trophy room. It's really just a set-up to get Harry and his friends in trouble, and after narrowly escaping the clutches of Filch (Hogwarts' caretaker), Harry, Ron, Hermione and Neville end up in the forbidden third-floor corridor where they come face-to-face with a monstrous three-headed dog who is sitting on a trapdoor. Back in the safety of the dormitory, Harry begins to suspect that the dog is guarding the secret package from vault 713.

WEST HAM SOCCER TEAM (PAGE 144)
Dean Thomas (one of Ron and Harry's roommates) has a poster of the West Ham Soccer team on their dorm wall. Of course, Dean—along with the original U.K. edition of the book—would actually call West Ham a football team. Indeed, West Ham United is one of London's several professional football teams, and we Americans can comfort ourselves that Ron Weasley, Quidditch fanatic, apparently knows just as little about British football as we do!

CANE (PAGE 150)
A thin pliable wooden cane used to beat unruly students. Caning,

as a form of corporal punishment, was commonplace in British schools in years past. My husband claims that he was on the receiving end of many a caning as a teenager at the Blue Coat School in Liverpool, him being one of those unruly sorts. Luckily for Harry and kids everywhere today, canings (and their U.S. cousin, paddlings) have been retired from the school systems.

FIFTH YEAR (PAGE 150)

A fifth year student (age 15-16) is in his or her fifth grade of secondary school, equivalent to our tenth grade. Oliver Wood, the captain of Gryffindor's Quidditch team, is a fifth year student in *Sorcerer's Stone*.

BIN (PAGE 151)

Also called a rubbish bin. To us, it's just a trash can.

STEAK AND KIDNEY PIE (PAGE 152)

Another British delicacy. Lovely on the outside (think our chicken pot pie) but a little scary on the inside. It is exactly how it sounds. Baked pastry filled with chopped steak and kidney and smothered in gravy. To be fair, it might actually be good. Harry and Ron certainly seem to be enjoying it and before he was a vegetarian, my husband claimed it was very nice. But the truth is, I've never been quite brave enough to try one.

BOGIES (PAGE 157)

The Curse of the Bogies is one of Quirrell's magical spells. A bogy or bogey (pronounced boe-gee with the stress on the first syllable) is a goblin or evil spirit. Their bogeyman is our boogieman. But for them, it has an even grosser meaning. A bogey (not a booger) is what little British kids (and surely some older ones) pick out of their noses.

– CHAPTER 10 –
HALLOWEEN

CHAPTER SUMMARY:

Harry receives his first broomstick, a Nimbus Two Thousand, and Oliver Wood teaches him the rules of Quidditch. After Charms class, Ron hurts Hermione's feelings and discovers she has gone to cry in the girl's bathroom. Shrugging it off, Ron and Harry join the others for the big Halloween feast. But the feast is short-lived. A troll has been spotted in the castle and students are ordered to return to their dormitories. En route, Harry remembers Hermione, all alone in the bathroom. Harry and Ron sneak to the bathroom, have a big fight with the troll and save Hermione's life. The experience seals the friendship among the three of them.

PLAYED FOR ENGLAND (PAGE 170)

When Wood says Charlie Weasley could have "played for England," he means Charlie was so good he could have made the national Quidditch team. In this context, Quidditch takes after the British soccer model. The national soccer (or football) team of England consists of the best players in the country who are 'capped' or picked from their local organizations to play against other national teams throughout the world in the World Cup and other competitions. An honor for sure, but Charlie had to go off and chase dragons.

TAP (PAGE 175)

A faucet. We often use the words interchangeably but they do not. Primarily, they say 'tap' to mean 'faucet.' This is what Harry throws against the wall in the bathroom to distract the troll from killing Hermione.

CATCH HIM A TERRIBLE BLOW (PAGE 176)

If the troll is about to "catch" Harry "a terrible blow," it just means that the big smelly creature is about to club Harry good. Luckily for Harry, wizard Ron is standing by.

– CHAPTER 11 –
QUIDDITCH

CHAPTER SUMMARY:
Harry begins to suspect that Snape is after the secret package guarded by the three-headed dog. His suspicions grow stronger when during Harry's first Quidditch match (Gryffindor vs. Slytherin), Harry's broom is sabotaged. With magical help from Hermione, Harry regains control of his Nimbus Two Thousand and goes on to capture the Golden Snitch and win the match. Later, Hagrid accidentally lets it slip that a man named Nicolas Flamel has something to do with the secret package that's hidden under the trapdoor and that the three-headed dog that's guarding it is named Fluffy.

WORLD CUP (PAGE 181)
The Quidditch World Cup is obviously inspired by the Soccer World Cup (called the Football World Cup by everyone in the world except us). Both are sporting events where national teams play each other to determine which team is the best in the world. Like the Soccer World Cup, the Quidditch World Cup is an honest to good-ness global competition, unlike our World Series where American teams only play each other (and sometimes the Canadians).

JAM JAR (PAGE 181)
A jar that contains British jam. But 'jam jar' is also a shorthand for 'glass jar'—like the kind American kids catch lightning bugs in (before they humanely release them).

BLASTED (PAGE 182)

When Professor Snape calls Fluffy a "blasted thing," he doesn't mean that the three-headed dog was shot out of a cannon. 'Blasted' is a common exclamation of frustration or annoyance. His 'blasted thing' translates to our 'darned thing.'

PITCH (PAGE 184)

At Hogwarts, the pitch is the field over which Quidditch is played. It's a grass surface surrounded by stands for spectators. In the British Muggle world, a soccer field is called a football pitch.

SIXTH YEAR (PAGE 185)

A sixth year student (age 16-17) is in his or her sixth grade of secondary school, equivalent to our eleventh grade. Marcus Flint, the captain of Slytherin's Quidditch team, is a sixth year student in *Sorcerer's Stone*.

BELTING ALONG (PAGE 186)

Lee Jordan, the Quidditch commentator, describes Angelina Johnson as "belting along" down the Quidditch pitch. Translated, it means that she is hauling butt down the field. But "belting along" isn't a phrase reserved only for sporting events. It's an expression that can be used to describe anyone who is moving quickly. For example, it's easy to imagine Mrs. Weasley belting along after one of her mischievous sons.

SEND HIM OFF, REF (PAGE 188)

This is exactly what it sounds like. Kick that guy out of the game! Dean Thomas yells this after Harry has been fouled by Marcus Flint. He would just as likely shout this during a West Ham football game.

CHAPPIE (PAGE 192)

Diminutive of chap. Chappie is a colloquial term for man, boy, fella or bloke (see *bloke*). The "Greek chappie" Hagrid bought Fluffy from at the pub was just some Greek guy he met there.

– CHAPTER 12 –
THE MIRROR OF ERISED

CHAPTER SUMMARY:

On Christmas morning at Hogwarts, Harry receives an anonymous package that contains his father's old invisibility cloak. After a day of Christmas fun, Harry sneaks out under his new cloak and finds an old ornate mirror in which he sees his family—dead relatives, including his parents, who wave to him. The next night, Ron looks into the same mirror and sees a reflection of himself as head boy and Quidditch captain. On Harry's third visit to the mirror, Dumbledore is waiting for him. He warns Harry that the mirror (called the Mirror of Erised) shows each person their deepest desire and can leave them living in a dream world. By the way, have you noticed what Erised spells backwards?

TREAT (PAGE 196)

When something "looks a treat," that means it looks beautiful or nice. It's how Hagrid describes the Great Hall.

FESTOONS (PAGE 196)

The Great Hall looks a treat because it is decorated for Christmas. These decorations include festoons that, in this instance, are long chains of holly and mistletoe that hang down in curves along the walls. Festoons can also be made of such materials as leaves, flowers or ribbons.

TOASTING FORK (PAGE 199)

Like a fondue fork, this is a long-handled, pronged metal instrument used to toast bread over a fire. Harry and Ron use them to toast marshmallows and English muffins over the Gryffindor fire.

ENGLISH MUFFINS (PAGE 199)

First of all, because they're English, the English don't call these English muffins. Get it? But the muffins that Harry and Ron are toasting are slightly different from the ones we call English muffins. When you pull them apart, they are smooth on the inside, unlike ours that are irregular and covered with little holes. In the UK, the ones that have those nooks and crannies are called crumpets.

FIFTY PENCE PIECE (PAGE 200)

A pence is a British penny. Add fifty of them together and you get fifty pence or half a pound. A fifty pence piece is like our fifty-cent coin, except that it's in everyday use (like a quarter over here). Also, it has a queen on it. In exchange-rate terms, it's worth a little less than a dollar. How generous of the Dursleys to send this as Harry's only Christmas gift?! They might as well have included a lump of coal.

FROG-MARCHED (PAGE 203)

Originally, this term applied to a prisoner when he was carried face down by four people who each held a different limb. In the case of Fred and George "frog marching" Percy to Christmas dinner, it's more likely that the twins have grabbed Percy by each arm and are hurrying him toward the Great Hall. What a pair of twins won't do for a little brotherly love on Christmas day!

CHRISTMAS DINNER (PAGE 203)

Think our Thanksgiving Dinner and you've got it. Turkey, stuffing (they don't say dressing), cranberries, potatoes, etc. This is their big turkey meal of the year. The Brits don't celebrate Thanksgiving (of course they don't, when you think about it!). In the Christmas days of Charles Dickens in the 19th century, it was the goose (not the turkey) that was cooked. Christmas dinner is served in households before or after the Queen's speech (a televised speech to the nation by the monarch at 3pm every Christmas day).

CHIPOLATAS (PAGE 203)
Small spicy sausages. They are either served on their own (like at the Hogwarts feast) or cut up and cooked into the stuffing.

CRACKERS (PAGE 203)
These are fantastic and we don't have anything like them. A cracker is party favor that's traditionally placed to the side of each plate at Christmas dinner. It is made of a thin cardboard tube (about six inches long), which is wrapped in colorful crepe paper that twists at the ends. Inside the tube there is a little bit of explosive and when you pull the ends apart, the house blows up. No, just kidding. It only makes a small explosive pop.

Once opened, the cracker releases its prizes: a paper crown (which you must wear throughout dinner), a fortune or joke (like the kind in a fortune cookie) and a little plastic toy (no better than the ones in Crackerjack boxes). Of course, what I'm describing is the harmless Muggle cracker. The wizard version sounds downright lethal.

CHRISTMAS PUDDING (PAGE 203)
A traditional British dessert served after Christmas dinner. Made of flour, nuts, dried fruit, alcohol and suet (a hard fat from the loins or kidneys of cattle or sheep), Christmas pudding is dark brown in color and looks something like our fruitcake. Steamed in a bowl in the oven, this dessert is served on a plate. One achieves this transfer by turning the bowl over, releasing its contents onto the plate (like you would with a Jell-O mold).

Now, here's the good part. An adult douses the dessert with brandy (or some other alcohol) and sets a match to it. And presto—

you've got a flaming Christmas pudding. It's beautiful but a little scary the first time you see it. My advice, keep your distance because it flames up very fast and you don't want to lose any eyelashes.

After the flame has burnt itself out (and not before!), the pudding is cut into individual pieces and covered with white sauce—a mixture of butter, sugar and alcohol (cognac or brandy). The sauce melts into the pudding giving off a wonderful aromatic smell.

My friend Margaret Anne has a wonderful memory of growing up in South Africa (once a British colony), and finding coins in her Christmas pudding. It's an old tradition to cook a few coins into the dessert (mostly for the benefit of children) so they can delight in discovering them while eating. At this particular Hogwarts' Christmas, it is Percy who comes up with the cash.

CRUMPETS (PAGE 204)

A crumpet is a soft cake mixture made with yeast (to make it rise) which is cooked on a griddle, or bought packaged from the store. They look like half of our English muffin (with the little holes) but are chewier, doughier and thicker. Usually served for breakfast or as part of afternoon tea, crumpets can be served with butter, cream or jam (or all three). Yummy good.

CHRISTMAS CAKE (PAGE 204)

A rich fruitcake covered with marzipan and a hard white icing (they don't say frosting). Unlike a Christmas pudding, which is steamed, a cake is baked. Years ago, this was also the kind of cake traditionally served at British weddings (until they wised up and realized nobody likes fruitcake).

– CHAPTER 13 –
NICOLAS FLAMEL

CHAPTER SUMMARY:

Harry finally discovers the identity of the mysterious Nicolas Flamel. He's the "only known maker of the Sorcerer's Stone." The Stone's powers include turning metals to gold and producing an elixir that gives the drinker everlasting life. Harry is sure that Fluffy is guarding this Stone. At his next Quidditch match, Harry catches the Golden Snitch and wins the game for Gryffindor. Later that night, a suspicious Harry follows Snape into the Forbidden Forest where he sees the teacher threaten Professor Quirrell. Harry thinks that Snape wants Quirrell to help him steal the Sorcerer's Stone.

CHRISTMAS HOLIDAYS (PAGE 215)

Christmas vacation. Like ours, their Christmas break lasts about two weeks, starting before Christmas and ending after New Years. For obvious reasons, Harry has chosen to spend this Christmas holiday at Hogwarts.

DEVON (PAGE 220)

Nicolas Flamel and his wife Perenelle are said to live in the English county of Devon. Located in the country's southwest peninsula, Devon is bordered by the county of Cornwall to the west and the counties of Somerset and Dorset to the east. To the north, its coast is situated along the Bristol Channel, to the south, Devon abuts the English Channel. There are many prehistoric sites in Devon including Kent's Cavern (one of the earliest known British dwellings) and Hembury Fort (an Iron Age hill fort). In the higher altitudes of the granite plateau of Dartmoor National Park, many Bronze Age remains have been found.

In the 7th century, the Saxons invaded and conquered the area of Devon. The county or shire (which was established in the 8th century) suffered repeated raids from the Danish until it was taken over by William the Conqueror in 1068.

Today, the most important industry in Devon is agriculture, including dairy farming. Devonshire clotted cream, which Brits enjoy with their afternoon tea, is produced there. Also, with its scenic interior and beautiful coasts, Devon attracts lots of tourists. The district of Torbay, on the southern coast, is one of England's most popular vacation destinations.

Sounds like a beautiful place for the Flamels to reside in their *very* old age.

– Chapter 14 –
Norbert The Norwegian Ridgeback

Chapter Summary:

Harry, Ron and Hermione learn that the Sorcerer's Stone is guarded by much more than just Fluffy. Each professor, including Snape, has performed a different enchantment to provide the Stone with added protection. Meanwhile, Hagrid receives an illegal dragon egg from a stranger in the village. After it hatches and Malfoy finds out about the dragon (named Norbert), Ron enlists his brother Charlie's help to smuggle Norbert to Romania. Ron ends up in the hospital wing after receiving a nasty bite from Norbert, so Harry and Hermione make the midnight rendezvous with Charlie's friends at the top of Hogwarts' tallest tower. The plan goes off without a hitch until Harry and Hermione re-enter the castle and run into Filch.

Second Year (page 229)
A second year student (age 12-13) is in his or her second grade of secondary school, equivalent to our seventh grade.

Easter Holidays (page 229)
Another break in the school year. It's like our spring break but theirs is a week longer than ours, which seems most unfair.

Rabbitin' About It (page 230)
This is an idiomatic expression which means blabbing about it.

Hagrid doesn't want Harry, Ron and Hermione yakking or rabbitin' about the Sorcerer's Stone in front of other students. It's supposed to be a secret!

BACK GARDEN (PAGE 230)
Back yard. Not a good place to keep a dragon.

WELSH (PAGE 231)
We discover that one breed of wild dragon in the United Kingdom is called the "Common Welsh Green" so it's a safe bet that it comes from Wales, a small country which adjoins England to the west. Famous Welshmen and women include Catherine Zeta Jones, Anthony Hopkins and the poet, Dylan Thomas.

Although the Welsh speak English, it's not technically their native language. Cymraeg (what they call their language) is derived from a form of Celtic language called Brythonic. About one-fifth of the Welsh can speak Cymraeg these days but very few speak Welsh and no English. In past decades, the Welsh have worked hard to keep their language and culture alive. This is reflected in the roadway signs throughout the country that are written in both English and Welsh.

The name Wales comes from an Old English word that means 'foreigner' and was given to them by the Anglo-Saxons who invaded Britain long ago. But the Welsh name for their country is Cymru, which means 'compatriots.'

HEBRIDEAN (PAGE 231)
Hebridean Blacks would be dragons from the Hebrides—a group of more than forty islands off the northwest coast of Scotland (the country in the U.K. that is north of England.) The Hebrides are divided into the Inner Hebrides and Outer Hebrides.

The Scottish speak English like the rest of the Brits but the former national language of Scotland was Scottish Gaelic. Like Cymraeg in Wales, Scottish Gaelic was derived from the Celtic languages.

Today, Scottish Gaelic is strongest in the Outer Hebrides. But that doesn't mean that many people speak it. Nowadays, only a few of the Hebrides islands are inhabited by humans. They say it is because of economic reasons but I think that it's just too ruddy cold up there!

STOAT SANDWICHES (PAGE 231)

Hagrid certainly eats some weird things and stoat sandwiches are no exception. Stoat (or ermine) is a type of weasel found in the Arctic, North America, Europe and even North Africa. They are called stoats in the summer when their fur is brown and ermine in the winter when their fur turns white. (How bizarre is that?) Ermine is a very valuable fur and at one time only royalty was allowed to wear it. But as for eating?

TARTAN (PAGE 240)

A woman who wears a tartan robe and has a name like McGonagall is most certainly of Scottish heritage. McGonagall is a Scottish name and the tartan is part of Scotland's Highland dress that goes back centuries. Tartans are crosscheck patterns woven into woolen cloth. This fabric is used to make kilts and other clothing. Originally designed as emblems for families and clans, tartans can represent almost any group or country today (as long as they are on good terms with the Scots!) In general, we think of tartans as plaid patterns that are more about fashion than family identification.

CHEERY LOT (PAGE 241)

A happy bunch. The kind of friends that Charlie Weasley would have.

– CHAPTER 15 –
THE FORBIDDEN FOREST

⚡

CHAPTER SUMMARY:

The antics of the previous night land Harry, Hermione, Malfoy and Neville (who tried to warn them but got caught) in detention. This detention takes place in the Forbidden Forest where they have to search for a wounded unicorn. The spooky night culminates with Harry finding the unicorn (which is dead) along with a hooded figure drinking its blood. When the hooded figure strikes, Harry is rescued by a centaur who says that the figure is a weakened but still dangerous Lord Voldemort. At the castle, Harry tells Ron and Hermione he thinks Voldemort drank the unicorn's blood to keep himself alive long enough for Snape to steal him the Sorcerer's Stone, which would bring Voldemort back to power and give him immortality.

IN ONE GO (PAGE 245)

Harry thinks he must be the only Gryffindor ever to lose 150 points "in one go," which happened when Harry got detention. This means he lost all those points in one shot or one fell swoop—something even Fred and George haven't managed to do.

SACKED (PAGE 247)

You don't get fired from a job in the U.K., you get "sacked." This usage comes from 17th century France where workmen carried tools to their jobs in sacks or bags. When they got laid off, they had to depart with their sacks. Thus, to be removed from employment came to mean 'to be sacked.'

– CHAPTER 16 –
THROUGH THE TRAPDOOR

CHAPTER SUMMARY:

During exams, Harry lives in fear that Voldemort will be brought back to power and come after him. When Dumbledore is called away to London, Harry believes this is the perfect opportunity for Snape to go after the Sorcerer's Stone. Armed with information from Hagrid on how to get past Fluffy, Harry, Ron and Hermione sneak to the third floor corridor and go through the trapdoor. But it is clear that someone has entered before them. As they hurry toward the Stone, they are challenged by many enchantments meant to guard it. In the end, only one of them can enter the last chamber so it is left to Harry to proceed alone.

SNUFFBOX (PAGE 262)

A snuffbox is a small decorated box designed to hold a powdered type of tobacco called snuff. In the 17th century, sniffing snuff became common in Britain and as the practice became popular in other countries, the demand for these little ornamental boxes grew. Some were small enough to fit into the pocket of a vest. Others were larger and would be displayed on tabletops. These boxes were made by artisans who specialized in making miniatures that could be quite elaborate and valuable. In the 18th century, some snuffboxes were even worn as jewelry.

BATTY (PAGE 263)

Though we might use the word 'batty,' which means insane or eccentric, the Brits say it much more than we would. And it's the perfect word to describe crazy old wizards who might come up on a History of Magic exam.

CHAPTER 17

THE MAN WITH TWO FACES

CHAPTER SUMMARY:

Harry enters the last chamber alone to see Professor Quirrell, not Snape, already inside. Quirrell was the one trying to kill Harry all along. The Mirror of Erised allows Harry to know where the sorcerer's stone is before Quirrell does. But before he can do anything about it, Quirrell unwraps his turban to reveal another face on the back of his head—that of Lord Voldemort who can only take form when sharing another's body. Voldemort orders Quirrell to kill Harry and a deadly struggle ensues. Harry awakens in the hospital wing to learn that Dumbledore showed up just in time to save him but that the bodiless Voldemort got away. Later, Gryffindor wins the house cup as a result of the bravery of Harry and his friends.

FUSSING ABOUT (PAGE 304)

Harry's arrival in the Great Hall is delayed by the "fussing about" of Madam Pomfrey. This is another one of those idiomatic phrases that the British use often. It means to show unnecessary or excessive concern or attention to something. In this case that something is Harry.

WAFFLE (PAGE 304)

Dumbledore's "wheezing waffle" has nothing to do with an asthmatic breakfast. Instead he is merely asking the students to indulge him while he launches into what he warns will be a lengthy and aimless dialogue. Of course, his speech turns out to be anything but waffle. In fact, it's of great importance to the Gryffindors to whom he awards the house cup!

WARDROBES (PAGE 307)

When I was a little kid, I thought *The Lion, the Witch and the Wardrobe* (another famous British children's book) meant the lion, the witch and all of her clothes. Of course, I was wrong. Because this kind of wardrobe is a free standing cabinet for holding clothes—what we more customarily call an armoire. But the British would also describe a regular clothes closet as a wardrobe. It's where Harry and the others keep their clothes at Hogwarts.

TOILETS (PAGE 307)

I know you know what a toilet is but in the U.K., the word 'toilet' can be used for more than just the porcelain thing you sit on. It can also mean the bathroom itself. For instance, at Hogwarts, they would say the girl's toilet instead of the girl's bathroom. And when Neville's lost toad is found in the toilets, it's probably discovered in a bathroom, not in a toilet bowl.

This leads us to the all-important subject of bathroom slang. Brits often refer to the bathroom by its popular slang name—'the loo.' No one knows exactly where this word originates but some theorize that 'loo' comes from the trade name 'Waterloo' which was a type of iron toilet tank or cistern made in the early 20th century. But my husband suggests that it's called the loo because it rhymes with poo. (I promise I'm not married to a five-year-old!)

A more rude slang term for the bathroom is the 'bog' and I would refrain from using it in polite company. (Of course I learned this lovely word from the not-five-year-old mentioned above.)

In more formal places like restaurants, they would probably put the slang aside and refer to the bathroom as the 'ladies' or the 'gents.'

And with this delightful definition of the toilet, we now close the book on *Harry Potter and the Sorcerer's Stone!*

-Part Two-

Harry Potter

AND THE
CHAMBER OF
SECRETS

CHAPTER 1

THE WORST BIRTHDAY

⊙─⊙

CHAPTER SUMMARY:
On Harry's twelfth birthday, there is no celebration in the Dursley house. Harry spends the day slaving away doing chores for Aunt Petunia as punishment for using the threat of magic to tease Dudley. That night, instead of enjoying a birthday cake, Harry is banished to his bedroom with a sandwich while the Dursleys greet dinner guests who are potential clients for Uncle Vernon. When Harry enters his bedroom, he sees a stranger sitting on his bed.

LOUNGE (PAGE 5)
When Aunt Petunia says she will be waiting for their dinner guests in the lounge, she means she will be in the living room. In a British home, the living room and family room are usually the same room, meaning there's probably a TV in there. It's also the place where they would entertain guests.

TOO RIGHT (PAGE 7)
Means 'darn straight' or 'you're not kidding.' Uncle Vernon uses 'too right' to confirm what Harry already knows. That he is to stay in his room, hidden from their guests during the dinner party. And there are to be no ifs, ands or buts about it.

DINNER JACKETS (PAGE 7)
Black tuxedo jackets. This must be some swanky dinner party

if Uncle Vernon and Dudley are renting (or as the Brits would say, hiring) tuxedos just to entertain at home. Sounds a little ridiculous but who are we to try and understand the Dursleys?

GARDEN BENCH (PAGE 7)

Okay, a garden bench would be found where? For those of you who have read the first part of this book (and I hope that's all of you!), it would be located in the garden (which we would call the yard). And the kind of benches traditionally found in British back yards would be made of wood or cast iron.

PUDDING (PAGE 10)

In years past, the word 'pudding' was used to specifically describe a spongy dessert made with suet. Like Christmas pudding, English pudding is prepared in a bowl and then steamed in the oven. After it is done, the bowl is turned over onto a plate where the pudding is released and the bowl is discarded. Now you've got a sort of upside down cake in the shape of the bowl in which it was cooked.

As we have learned, this is not a cake because: 1) a pudding is steamed, not baked, and 2) a pudding is made with suet which makes it heavier and more dense (remember, suet is that lovely hard animal fat we discussed in the section on Christmas pudding). But unlike Christmas pudding, which is dark and studded with fruit like a fruitcake, regular pudding is yellow and spongy. It's pretty plain so you can jazz it up by cooking it with treacle or jam (which makes it treacle pudding or jam pudding). Then, you slice the pudding into pieces and serve it in individual dessert bowls. Topping pudding with custard is a popular option—especially for people who are married to me.

The dessert I've just described is still called pudding in the U.K.; however, nowadays pudding is most often bought pre-cooked and packaged and ready to eat from a supermarket like Tesco. Also, the word 'pudding' itself has evolved to describe almost any type of dessert—from apple pie to chocolate ice cream. Like our dessert, 'pudding' is what is served after dinner.

But this begs the question, when they eat that creamy wonderful stuff we call pudding, what do they call it? Our kind of pudding is usually marketed there under specific brand names such as Instant Whip or Angel Delight. But of course in the broader sense, because it is also a dessert, a Brit would still technically call our pudding, a 'pudding.'

SUGARED VIOLETS (PAGE 10)

These are tiny hard sugar candies that are colored purple and shaped into flowers. Sugared violets can be eaten alone as yummy snacks but in the case of Aunt Petunia's whipped cream and sugared violets pudding, the violets are sprinkled on top of a whipped cream dessert concoction.

– CHAPTER 2 –
DOBBY'S WARNING

CHAPTER SUMMARY:

Dobby, the house-elf of a prominent yet unnamed wizarding family, is waiting for Harry in his bedroom. He warns Harry not to return to Hogwarts because there is a terrible plot against him. When Harry doesn't comply with Dobby's wishes, the elf wreaks havoc by crashing Aunt Petunia's whipped cream and sugared violets pudding onto the kitchen floor. Then, an owl flies through the dining room window, sending their dinner guests screaming from the house. The owl carries a message for Harry which reveals to the Dursleys that Harry is not allowed to use magic outside of school. Empowered by this new information, Uncle Vernon locks Harry in his room and forbids him to go back to Hogwarts.

DOBBY-SPEAK (PAGE 12)

Dobby's speech patterns remind me of Yoda's from the *Star Wars* series. But picture an alternate reality where Yoda is part of the servant class of old London who doesn't have that wisdom thing down yet. In reality, Dobby's speech echoes Dickensian servant talk. Dickensian refers to Charles Dickens who is considered by many to be the greatest and most popular writer of the Victorian Age (remember, that means during the reign of Queen Victoria, 1837-1901). He often wrote about the plight of the underclass and the servant class in books like *A Christmas Carol*, *Oliver Twist* and *A Tale of Two Cities*. If you ever see an old British movie based on a Dicken's novel, you'll certainly hear some servant who talks like Dobby.

TOP OF MY YEAR (PAGE 15)

Over here in the U.S., we would say 'the head of the class' which of course means the person with the best grades in the school year. At Hogwarts, it's Hermione, not Harry, who's got the best marks in their year.

BANSHEE (PAGE 20)

I've heard people use the phrase 'screaming like a banshee' all my life but I must confess, until now I had no idea what a banshee really was. So for those of you who are also a little fuzzy on the banshee thing, here's my best attempt to define it. The word 'banshee' comes from Irish Folklore. Folklore, for your information, is simply the lore of a particular people (or folk) told in the oral tradition. Meaning, it's the stories and folk wisdom people told around campfires, in caves or wherever they where hanging out together. Folklore consists of stories that encompass the beliefs, customs and legends of a culture. Over centuries, folklore seeped into literature and was often transformed into mythology. In Irish Folklore, the banshee is a wailing, shrieking female spirit who does her screaming under the windows of a house where someone inside is close to death. So, technically, a banshee's wail is something that foreshadows death.

CAT-FLAP (PAGE 22)

A smaller version of our 'doggie door' that is primarily used by cats (or by the horrible Dursleys to slide meager meals to the imprisoned Harry). Evidently, British dogs do not have the luxury of tramping in and out of the house via doggie doors like many of their American cousins. That is unless they are little cat-size dogs that can squeeze through the cat flap.

FRUIT BAT (PAGE 22)

If Harry were to turn the Dursleys into fruit bats, they would become small tropical fruit-eating bats that belong to the family Pteropodidae. But my guess is that the family Dursley wouldn't last a day on only fruit!

– CHAPTER 3 –
THE BURROW

CHAPTER SUMMARY:

Ron, George and Fred arrive at Harry's window in their father's enchanted flying Muggle car and spring Harry and Hedwig from their imprisonment. At sunrise, they touch down at the Weasley's house (the Burrow) where Mrs. Weasley reads them the riot act for sneaking out, then welcomes Harry to their home and feeds them breakfast. Exhausted, the boys want to sleep but are instructed to de-gnome the yard first. Later, Mr. Weasley comes home from work at the Ministry of Magic and is pleased to finally meet Harry. When Harry sees Ron's room, he reveals to his friend that the Burrow is the best house he has ever seen.

PUT YOUR FOOT DOWN (PAGE 27)

The Weasley boys have come to rescue Harry by flying the family car up to Harry's window but Uncle Vernon does his best to stop them. In their attempt to get away, Ron tells his brother Fred (who is driving the car) to "put his foot down." We would simply yell, "step on it, Fred!" Either way, they mean to put the pedal to the metal and get the heck out of there.

DODGY (PAGE 28)

If something is dodgy, it is suspect or, like Fred says, 'fishy.' A whole host of things can be dodgy in the British world, from five-day-old meat to a too-good-to-be-true business deal. In this case, it's Dobby's story that sounds "definitely dodgy." Dodgy can also refer to something that has been stolen (or lifted, or pinched, or nicked, as the Brits might say).

MANOR (PAGE 29)

Harry assumes that Draco Malfoy lives on a manor which is the kind of place where one would have a house-elf like Dobby. An English manor is a large estate. Think *Downton Abbey*. Think lots of land and servants. The mansion or manor house is where the owners of such an estate live (and apparently torture their house-elves).

TEA SET (PAGE 31)

I know a lot of families have tea sets in this country but certainly not all of them. That's where the Brits are different. I would be willing to bet that almost every British household owns some sort of tea set, even if it's merely a couple of cups and saucers with a teapot. (Sadly, this is becoming less true with the younger dunk-a-teabag-in-a-mug generation.)

The basic tea set includes six cups and saucers, a teapot, a milk jug (remember, they drink their tea with milk), a sugar bowl and a tray on which all this stuff can rest. The ones made of china, porcelain or ceramic usually come in matching designs. However, a formal teapot, milk jug and sugar bowl can also be made of silver (a silver service) and would be accompanied by china cups and saucers.

OTTERY ST. CATCHPOLE (PAGE 31)

Like other town names in *Harry Potter* (Little Whinging, anyone?), Ottery St. Catchpole is one of those places that sounds cleverly invented. This three-barreled, somewhat exotic name (to us) is not untypical of the kind of name given to many British towns and villages (like Newton-le-Willows and Bury St. Edmunds). And it has the quaint and quirky sound of a place where the quaint and quirky Weasleys might live. So why do I think Ottery St. Catchpole is a made up place? Well, I've heard of St. Patrick and St. Theresa but tell me honestly, have you ever heard of St. Catchpole?

THE BURROW (PAGE 32)

A burrow as you probably know is a place where rabbits live. Now I'm not calling the Weasleys rabbits but you've got to admit they have a lot of children!

Many middle class homes in the U.K. are given names by their owners and The Burrow wouldn't be an unusual one, especially for a cozy family house like the Weasleys have. Other little plaques or signs erected outside of homes might boast names like Seaview (for a coastal home) or Dunroamin (named by the owner who has finally settled down in a home and has 'done roaming').

BREAD AND BUTTER (PAGE 35)

I know you know what bread and butter are. And I know that we have lots of bread and butter in this country. Yet, I cannot refrain from telling you that the British eat bread and butter like it's some kind of sporting event. And there's a good reason. It's the butter. So creamy, so delicious, British butter is the best butter I have ever tasted.

NIGHTDRESS (PAGE 35)

Nightgown. What Ginny is wearing.

WOE BETIDE YOU (PAGE 36)

When Mrs. Weasley exclaims, "Woe betide you if there's a single gnome (left) in that garden," she's telling the boys, "God help you if you don't remove every single one of them from the yard." It's a motherly threat that warns of big trouble if they don't do what she says—pronto.

GERROFF ME! (PAGE 37)

Even though in this case it's a gnome that screams, "Gerroff me!" lots of British kids (especially from the North) would say, "get off me" exactly the same way. Here, J.K. Rowling is just spelling it out for us phonetically (the way it sounds).

– CHAPTER 4 –
AT FLOURISH AND BLOTTS

CHAPTER SUMMARY:

Harry and the Weasleys (even Ginny) receive letters from Hogwarts with their course book requirements for the coming school year. Using floo powder, they all travel to Diagon Alley where they meet Hagrid, and Hermione and her parents. At the bookstore, Flourish and Blotts, Gilderoy Lockhart breaks from his book signing to get his photo taken with Harry and announces that he will be taking the position of the Defense Against the Dark Arts teacher at Hogwarts this year. A few minutes later, Lucius Malfoy picks up one of Ginny's second hand books and uses it to taunt the poorer Mr. Weasley. A fight ensues that takes Hagrid to break it up. After leaving the bookstore, they travel back to the Burrow by floo powder.

YETI (PAGE 44)

A yeti is the Tibetan name for a mythical big-foot like creature rumored to inhabit the Himalayas (rumored is the key word here). It's what we call the Abominable Snowman, an enormous humanoid snow monster that shows up on TV from amateur videos every now and then. What relevance does a yeti have in a book on British slang and customs? Well, the answer to that could be a bit dodgy so let's just say that my English niece spotted a yeti on her last trip to the Outer Hebrides which I feel gives me every right to include it in this book (can anyone else feel my nose growing?). But the real question here is does anyone actually believe that a coward like

Gilderoy Lockhart spent a "Year with the Yeti?" I doubt he spent a minute with one.

BUTTER DISH (PAGE 44)

The butter dish on the Weasley table is most likely made of ceramic, glass or metal. It's a flat dish with a lip around the edges and a cover with a high lid. It can come in a larger size for half pound butter slabs or a smaller one to fit our regular butter sticks. And—shocker!—in most British homes, they don't keep the butter in the fridge.

LOVELY (PAGE 44)

My, how they love this word. For Percy, it's a "lovely day" he's describing but trust me, anything that is nice or beautiful or pleasing is 'lovely' to the Brits. I would bet that it's one of the top ten most used words in the English (and I mean British-English) language.

YOUR ONE (PAGE 45)

Interchangeable with 'yours.' You could say, 'give me yours' or 'give me your one.' It's all the same and sounds perfectly normal to the non-American ear.

LOVE FROM (PAGE 45)

When I first started getting notes from my English niece, her sign off (Love from Gemma) always made me smile. The combination of 'love' and 'from' felt strange to me but I found it endearing. So it makes perfect sense (to them) that Hermione would sign off in the same manner when writing to her friends Ron and Harry.

O.W.Ls (ORDINARY WIZARDING LEVELS) (PAGE 46)

In this case, O.W.L.s do not refer to Harry's pet owl, Hedwig, or the Weasley's owl, Errol, but to something infinitely less pleasant—exams.

Under the definition for secondary school in Part One of this book, we learned about O Levels (short for General Certificate of Secondary Education Ordinary Level). To recap, at Percy's age (16), students in real British schools take their O Levels—a series of tests, usually in eight or more subjects. You have to pass a certain number of these tests to move on into the 6th Form (the last two years of high school).

So, let's say our friend Nigel took ten O Level tests but only passed six of them. It would be said that he 'got six O Levels.' Does that make it easier to understand what it means when Fred and George say that two of their brothers got twelve O.W.L.s each? Based on the assumption that the O.W.L.s in the *Chamber of Secrets* are modeled after O Levels, Bill and Percy must have passed twelve tests. In real British schools, twelve O Levels would be a remarkable amount to 'get.' This tells us that Bill and Percy are really smart—when it comes to course work, that is. Because we all know that Percy's not so bright when it comes to people.

MASTER (PAGE 51)

Did you wonder why Mr. Borgin addressed Draco's father as Mr. Malfoy and Draco as 'Master Malfoy' in his shop? That's because until a boy reaches eighteen, he is referred to as 'master' instead of 'mister.' Sure, it's an old fashioned, formal usage that you don't hear so often today. But surely old fashioned formal people would still employ it when addressing or talking about a young man. And in the mail, Draco would certainly receive many letters addressed to Master Draco Malfoy. (But who would want to write him anyway?)

TEN-POUND NOTES (PAGE 57)

Mr. Weasley exclaims that a ten-pound note is Muggle money—real British currency that is somewhat similar in size to our ten-dollar bill but is worth more because of the exchange rate. It is called a 'note' because that's what they call their paper money over there like we say 'bills' here. Their ten-pound note is now made of polymer, not paper. But that's not the only difference between their notes and ours.

Whereas the front of our bills sport the pictures of presidents and other noteworthy dead white men, the front of all British notes (no matter what denomination) display the likeness of Queen Elizabeth II. This will change when she dies and her son, Prince Charles ascends to the throne. Then he will appear on the money. Queen Elizabeth is the current monarch of the United Kingdom and was crowned after the death of her father, King George VI, in 1952. On the back of the current polymer ten-pound note is the image of another famous English woman—the author, Jane Austen. Born in 1775, Austen wrote many novels, including Sense and Sensibility (1811) and Pride and Prejudice (1813) which remain enormously popular, both to readers and to the fans of the movies and miniseries made from them.

Before the polymer notes, there were paper notes or bills like we have here. There was a design on the back side of a previous paper ten-pound British note that I found very interesting. It honored Charles Dickens and his 1836 book *The Pickwick Papers*. It included a portrait of Mr. Dickens along with an illustration of a cricket match described in his book which happens to be between the teams of Dingley Dell and all Muggleton!

But if the fronts of their notes are the same (except for the number which indicates their worth), you might be wondering how people easily tell them apart? The answer is easy and ingenious. Their notes come in different colors and sizes. Ten-pound notes feature one color scheme, twenty-pound notes another color scheme, etc. and vary slightly in size. It confuses Brits to no end to come to this country and have to use our money because it looks all the same to them. Green, green and more green. So don't use the word 'greenback' when talking to a Brit about money. They won't have the foggiest idea what you're talking about.

GAMBOL AND JAPES WIZARDING JOKE SHOP (PAGE 58)

The owners of this joke shop have names that summon the spirits of Europe's original gambollers and japesters—court jesters. Words like gambol (meaning to frolic or dance around playfully) and jape (meaning to jest or joke) often described the antic behavior of these playful fellows who entertained royalty from medieval times to the 17th century. Many jesters became quite famous: Robert Grene gambolled and japed for Queen Elizabeth I, and Muckle John gambolled and japed for Charles I. But that's where the laughter ended because Muckle John was the last royal court jester of England.

– CHAPTER 5 –

THE WHOMPING WILLOW

$$9\tfrac{3}{4}$$

CHAPTER SUMMARY:

After Harry's happy month at the Burrow, Mr. Weasley drives everyone to Kings Cross Station in his enchanted Ford Anglia to catch the Hogwarts Express. When the magical barrier on Platform Nine and Three-Quarters won't let Harry and Ron through, the boys decide to fly Ron's dad's car to Hogwarts. Upon arrival at school, they crash land into the Whomping Willow tree. After Harry and Ron escape from the car (and the willow), they watch the driverless Ford Anglia take off into the Forbidden Forest. The stunt lands Harry and Ron in detention but their antics earn them a grand welcome by their fellow Gryffindors.

TREACLE PUDDING (PAGE 65)

Wouldn't you just know that Mrs. Weasley could make terrific treacle pudding? But as mouthwatering as it is to Harry, it might taste a little strange to those of us on this side of the Atlantic.

If you have been reading this book carefully, you already know what a treacle pudding is. (Because I told you!) But for those of you who like to skip around, take the 'treacle' from the definition of treacle tart (a syrupy substance like molasses) and the 'pudding' from the section on pudding (a spongy cake made with suet), put them together and voila, you get the ever popular treacle pudding.

FORD ANGLIA (PAGE 66)

The Ford Anglia was a popular car in the U.K. during the 1950s and 60s. A small, four-door, boxy vehicle, the Anglia wouldn't cause people to think you were the richest family on the block but it would nevertheless do a fine job of getting you wherever you wanted to go.

Mr. Weasley's Ford Anglia would have the driver's seat on the right side of the car because Brits drive on the opposite side of the road to us! Whenever I ride in someone's car in the U.K. (I would never dare to drive there), I always experience at least one butt-clenching moment when I'm afraid we're going to get killed by oncoming traffic.

TOFFEES (PAGE 71)

With nothing to eat but toffees during the flight in the Ford Anglia, it's no wonder that Ron and Harry get thirsty. I imagine they would feel a little sick as well because English toffees are similar to what we call caramels—small pieces of chewy candy made of sugar and butter that stick to your stomach and your teeth. Think of the color and consistency of caramel covered apples (which by the way, they call toffee apples) and you'll get the idea. Toffee is much loved by the Brits but sometimes they get a taste for the exotic, and in those moments, I send my niece a bag of tootsie rolls. Because astonishingly, you can't buy tootsie rolls over there (at least you couldn't when she was little). And there, my friends, is an example of where we got it right. I'll take an American tootsie roll over an English toffee any day.

MOORS (PAGE 72)

For those of you who are… let's just call you more mature Harry Potter readers… you've probably read about the moors in English books like *Wuthering Heights* by Emily Bronte. The moors (or moorlands) are the romantic countryside where Cathy and Heathcliff fell in love. Moors are open, desolate stretches of land found in the Yorkshire region of England.

There are two kinds of moors: wet moors (also called bogs) and dry moors (where the lovely low flowering shrub called heather grows). So, which kind of moor are Harry and Ron flying over in the Ford Anglia? That would be the dry kind. We know this because the moor described in the book is said to be purplish. And there exists a type of heather called Scotch heather that just happens to be the color purple.

POST OFFICE TOWER (PAGE 79)

The *Evening Prophet* has printed several eyewitness reports of a "flying Ford Anglia." The first comes from London where Ron and Harry were spotted flying over the Post Office tower. Right away my mind conjured up the image of a medieval tower with turrets which happens to have a post office in it. But this Post Office tower is no Tower of London. Instead, it's a modern skyscraper made of steel, glass and concrete which sprouts a plethora of television and radio antennae from its rooftop.

NORFOLK (PAGE 79)

Another one of England's counties, Norfolk is located northeast of London and borders the North Sea. The county boasts a long rich history and artifacts from the Paleolithic, Mesolithic and Neolithic eras have been found there.

One of the most interesting characters to come out of Norfolk was Queen Boudicca (pronounced Boo-di-ca). She was the queen of the Iceni people who inhabited Norfolk two thousand years ago during the time Imperial Rome was conquering all of Europe including Great Britain. In 60 C.E., Boudicca led a revolt against the Romans. She and her warriors burned down the new Roman city of Londinium (later called London) and killed over 70,000 Roman soldiers, thus making a quite a name for herself, albeit a bloody one, in history. Sadly for Boudicca and the Britons she led, the Romans eventually defeated them and Queen Boudicca poisoned herself rather than be captured by her enemy.

But history always has a way of evening the score as evidenced by the fact that the British don't speak Latin today. Heck, even the Italians don't speak Latin today. But again, that is another story, which takes us far from Norfolk. What is pertinent here is that Harry and Ron fly over London before they reach Norfolk. That means that they are heading north.

PEEBLES (PAGE 79)

And heading north they are! I have long suspected that Hogwarts is located in Scotland (the northernmost country of the United Kingdom) and Peebles is the clue that finally confirms my suspicions because Peebles is a town smack dab in the middle of Scotland! Even though the Ford Anglia doesn't land in Peebles, it's a fair bet that it is going to land nearby. Because, frankly, once you get as north as Scotland, where else are you going to go? What this means for Harry and his friends is that Hogwarts winters are really cold. We're not talking London cold, but Edinburgh (the capital city of Scotland) cold. And that is without doubt as cold as you ever want to be.

CUSTARD TART (PAGE 82)

A small pastry shell (like a mini-pie crust) that is filled with egg custard. Whereas we can find custard tarts at some American bakeries, they are absolute staples in every British pastry shop and probably show up for dessert quite often at Hogwarts.

SUITS OF ARMOR (PAGE 83)

See *coats of armor.*

WATTLEBIRD (PAGE 84)

The password to the Gryffindor dormitory is wattlebird. A wattlebird is from the songbird family called Callaeidae of which there are three distinct species, although one of them is now extinct. They get their name from the 'wattles' or loose skin that forms at the corners of their mouths. Wattlebirds are only found in the forests of New Zealand, which is an island country southeast of Australia in the South Pacific. New Zealand leads us to another important subject which pertains to Great Britain and its political history. That is the Commonwealth.

To understand Great Britain, you need to have some understanding of the Commonwealth—an association of nations established in the early 20th century as a way for Great Britain to stay connected to the territories of its Empire that didn't want to remain territories any longer. These Commonwealth member countries are sovereign states that maintain a kind of friendship and cooperation with each other while allowing the British monarch (right now that's Queen Elizabeth II) to remain as their symbolic head. The Commonwealth is made up of countries from all over the world including New Zealand, Australia, Canada, India, Kenya, Barbados, to name a few. Currently, there are 53 country members of the British Commonwealth.

The Commonwealth exists today because of what existed before—the British Empire. After Queen Elizabeth I built a great navy that defeated the Spanish Armada in 1588, Britain emerged as the dominant imperial power among the European nations. And then they really went for it, conquering countries all over the world. Remember, we fought the Revolutionary War to get them out of this country.

By the 19th century, the British Empire reached its zenith by controlling a multitude of countries including India, Australia, many African nations and more. This was one big mighty empire I'm talking about. But like all empires, it overextended its reach and by the end of World War II, the British Empire began to crumble. The first to go was India. In 1947, Mahatma Gandhi's non-violent movement for Indian independence sent the British packing. It was only a matter of time before its other territories were released from the Empire's grip. (Sounds a bit like the *Star Wars* saga, right?) The Commonwealth exists today because of the relationships made during the time of the British Empire.

And that, my friends, concludes this definition of the wattlebird.

– CHAPTER 6 –
GILDEROY LOCKHART

CHAPTER SUMMARY:
On the first day of school at breakfast, Ron receives a Howler from his mother by owl post that scolds him for flying the Ford Anglia to Hogwarts. After lunch, a star-struck first year, Colin Creevey, asks Harry to pose for and sign a photograph. When Malfoy calls attention to this, Gilderoy Lockhart gets the wrong idea about Harry and lectures him about becoming too big-headed. Mortified, Harry skulks off to his Defense Against the Dark Arts class. There, Lockhart lets loose Cornish pixies for the students to recapture. The lesson is a total fiasco leaving Ron and Harry wondering if Lockhart is as accomplished as his books say he is.

KIPPERS (PAGE 86)

Now before you say some people in the U.S. eat kippers for breakfast, (although I haven't met many who do), let me explain that kippers are a much more common item on the British breakfast menu than they are on ours. A kipper is a fish, more specifically a herring, which is about six inches long and looks like an overgrown sardine. When you buy it from the grocery store, it comes smoked and salted. Then you fry it up in a frying pan and usually serve it with toast and butter (big surprise). For the hearty, kippers could even be part of what a Brit would call a 'fry up.' That's a meal of, you guessed it, fried stuff, usually for breakfast which could include fried eggs, fried tomatoes, fried mushrooms, fried baked beans, fried sausage, fried bread and black pudding. Don't know what black pudding is? If you really want to know—and frankly I don't think you *do* want to know—I'll tell you what a black pudding is: it's pig's blood. A whole lot of pig's blood, mixed with suet and oatmeal, stuffed into a casing of animal intestine, and then boiled until it solidifies into a sausage-like texture. Once cooled, it can be eaten cold but most Brits, probably because they feel the disgusto-meter is still a notch or two short of maxing out, slice it into patties and fry it, often in the same happily bubbling skillet full of lard that contains their eggs, bacon, mushrooms, tomatoes, and fried bread. Yum!

CHAPS (PAGE 90)

Not what an American cowboy wears on his legs, but a man, fella, bloke or boy. In other words, a 'chap' is a 'guy.' So why does Professor Sprout call her male *and* female students chaps? Because if you haven't learned it already, British slang is full of exceptions and informally addressing a group of any sex as chaps is one of them.

ETON (PAGE 94)

Eton is a town next to Windsor (less than an hour west of London), which is home to one of the largest and most exclusive private (or as they say, public) boarding schools in England— Eton. The school is idiosyncratically called Eton College but it is not a college in the way we would think of it. It is a secondary school that was established by King Henry VI in 1440 for boys. Today, Eton remains a school for boys (mostly rich ones) but unlike Hogwarts, these boys begin Eton at the age of thirteen. Windsor is the home of Windsor Castle, a favorite royal residence of the queen. This was where Prince Harry married the American, Meghan Markle.

When Justin Finch-Fletchley says his "name was down for Eton," that means he was accepted to Eton and could have gone there. This also tells us that Justin's parents are probably Muggles because Eton is definitely a Muggle school. It's the place where Princes William and Harry went to school.

SPELLOTAPE (page 95)

This is a play on words that is completely lost on American readers. But that's about to change! You know how we generally call clear tape by the brand name, Scotch tape? Well, the most popular brand name for such tape in Britain is 'Cellotape' (with that 'C' pronounced as an 'S'). Clearly, and cleverly, 'Spellotape' is its witchy equivalent.

FULL MARKS (PAGE 100)

When Gilderoy Lockhart gives Hermione "full marks," he's awarding her the top grade possible on the test he just made them take (if you can call that a real test). Idiomatically, full marks can also be an expression that simply means well done.

CORNISH PIXIES (PAGE 101)

Cornish pixies are supernatural creatures, akin to fairies, that dance in the moonlight and wreak havoc on innocent humans. They appear in the folklore of Cornwall (thus the name Cornish pixies), which is a county in the most southwest corner of England. Like most fairies, pixies are small in size, mischievous and sometimes dangerous (facts to which Lockhart's classroom can now attest!). They are thought to have pointed ears and to wear costumes of green. Pixies are especially naughty when it comes to travelers, whom they love to lead astray. When a person would become bewildered or lost, they would be what was called 'pixie-led.' From this term evolved the word 'pixilated' which means to be confused or bewildered in a more general sense.

Cornwall is a long peninsula that borders the Celtic Sea on one side and the English Channel on the other. Tintagel Castle, on the north coast of Cornwall, is thought by many to be the castle of the legendary King Arthur. So with all its beauty, beaches and history, it's no surprise that tourists flock to Cornwall when the weather is good. When there, they often purchase lucky charms that come in the form of small pixie figurines. But from what we've learned about pixies, does there seem anything remotely lucky about them to you?

BLIGHTERS (PAGE 101)

Rotters, cads, sods or gits. A blighter is a name you call someone who is a blight, one who exerts a negative or damaging influence on others. Lockhart calls his just-released pixies "tricky little blighters" and for perhaps the first time, we know that Gilderoy Lockhart is speaking the truth.

BUDGIES (PAGE 101)

Here is another bird that can connect us back to the Commonwealth because a budgie is an Australian parrot (Australia being the Commonwealth member, not the budgie). The proper name for a budgie is a budgerigar or a shell parakeet. Among the smallest of the parrots, budgies are often kept as pets. Fun fact: Budgies have monocular vision. This means they can see independently out of each eye and can even move their eyes in different directions.

J.K. Rowling compares the voices of the pixies to "a lot of budgies arguing" which makes total sense if you know that budgies are talking birds that love to live in flocks or groups. In the wild, budgies have light green and yellow markings but in captivity, they have been bred in many colors. They are favorite cage and show birds in England and my husband tells me there were budgies in many many British homes when he was growing up—which makes me want to yell: FREE THE BUDGIES!

NIP (PAGE 102)

Rhymes with kip and that in itself makes it one of my favorite words. When Lockhart asks our heroes to "nip (the pixies) back into their cage," he's using slang to cut down on the words it would take to tell them to quickly pop the little blighters back into their miniature jail cell. To 'nip' means to do something quickly and be done with it. If I had a nickel for every time my husband said, "I'll just nip down to the shops," I'd be...well...richer than I am now. Translated that means, "I'm going to hurry down to the store and be back in a few minutes." Fewer words, same meaning.

Chapter 7

Mudbloods and Murmurs

Chapter Summary:

At an early morning Gryffindor Quidditch practice, the Slytherin team shows up and reveals that their new seeker is none other than Draco Malfoy, and that Malfoy's father, Lucius, has bought every member of the Slytherin team a new Nimbus Two Thousand and One broomstick. It gets even worse when Malfoy calls Hermione a "Mudblood"—a very derogatory term to describe someone who was born a Muggle. When they arrive back at the castle, McGonagall assigns Harry and Ron their detention duties from the flying Ford Anglia incident. During this detention, Harry hears a menacing voice call out from somewhere within the walls of Hogwarts. It's a voice that only Harry can hear.

Changing Rooms (page 107)
When Harry dashes into the changing rooms to get away from Colin Creevy, he's merely escaping into what we call a locker room.

Fourth Year (page 107)
A fourth year student (ages 14-15) is in his or her fourth grade of secondary school which is equivalent to our ninth grade of high school. Alicia Spinnet, a Chaser on the Gryffindor Quidditch team, is a fourth year student in *Chamber of Secrets*.

Clear Off (page 110)
When Oliver Wood tells the Slytherins to "clear off," he means for

them to get off the field. This is a popular expression that is used generically to mean 'get lost' or 'get out of here,' especially when someone is angry.

LEERING TO A MAN (PAGE 110)

If the Slytherin team is "leering to a man," that means that they are leering in unison at the same someone or something. In this case, "to a man" is used idiomatically to mean 'everyone' and refers back to the people doing the leering, not the people being leered at. Without doubt, this is a weird one that even upon explanation sounds a little strange.

KELPIES (PAGE 114)

From Scottish folklore (or from the folklore of the land where we believe Hogwarts is located), a kelpie is a water spirit that appears in the form of a horse. Kelpies supposedly get pleasure from the drowning of travelers, which in my mind makes them much more sinister than the mischievous pixies who would merely delight in getting the same travelers lost. But on the positive side, kelpies are said to give occasional aid to millers by keeping their mill wheels turning during the night. (A miller is someone who runs a grain mill.)

The fact that Hagrid knows how to get such dangerous supernatural beasts out of a well gives us even more reason to admire the gifts of this gentle giant.

BANGIN' ON (PAGE 115)

When Hagrid says that Lockhart was banging on "about some banshee," he means that Lockhart was harping on about it in a manner that became tedious and annoying—adjectives that quite appropriately describe Gilderoy Lockhart, don't you think?

TREACLE FUDGE (PAGE 115)

You guessed it—this is fudge laced with treacle, or what we would think of as molasses flavored fudge. Are you starting to spot the treacle trend?

SHEPHERD'S PIE (PAGE 119)

During a bleak dinner before his detention, Harry eats a shepherd's pie—real honest-to-goodness British comfort food (although under the circumstances, it does little to comfort poor Harry). This is not a sweet dessert pie—nor, in case you were worried, is it made from shepherds—but is a wonderful warm savory dish. The recipe goes something like this:

- Before you start, cook up a batch of mashed potatoes and put aside.
- Then take out a pan and put it on the stove.
- Add 2 tbsp. oil and turn on the heat.
- Dice one onion and sauté it in the oil.
- Add one chopped clove of garlic and one chopped carrot.
- Increase heat.
- Then, add a pound of ground meat (usually this is lamb but you can use ground beef) and cook until brown.
- Add 2 tsp. curry paste or powder, 1/3 cup beef or lamb stock, a squirt of ketchup, 1 tsp. soy sauce, 1 whole diced tomato, 1/2 cup of peas.
- Into a separate cup, pour 1/2 cups of water and add a tbsp. or so of cornstarch to it. Stir until the mixture is smooth.
- Add the cornstarch and water to the cooking ingredients to help it thicken.
- Simmer for 5 minutes.
- After it cools for a few minutes, pour the mixture into a casserole dish.
- Then spread a thick layer of mashed potatoes on top of the lamb or beef mixture.
- Grate cheese all over the top of the potatoes.
- Put the casserole dish in the oven at 375 F and cook until the cheese begins to brown.

Now, get ready for a delightful culinary experience that's easy to make!

SCALAWAG (PAGE 119)

When Lockhart addresses Harry as a "scalawag," he's calling him a mischievous scamp or a good-for-nothing kid. After all, Harry *is* arriving for detention. Scalawag (or scallywag) is a word that originated in the U.S. where it became common slang in the 19th century. From here, it traveled to the British Isles. Before it was used on people, scalawag was a word that described underfed or poorly conditioned cattle.

Scalawag is one of those great words that sometimes falls out of fashion, which it did in the 20th century. But it has seen a revival in the home of my husband's birth, Liverpool, England. A modern-day scalawag—usually shortened to scally or scal—is a 'bit of a lad' or a 'cheeky chappy'— a teen or young adult who is charming trouble.

– CHAPTER 8 –
THE DEATHDAY PARTY

CHAPTER SUMMARY:

Instead of joining the other students for the Halloween feast, Harry, Ron and Hermione go to Nearly Headless Nick's Deathday Party in the Hogwart's dungeon. Many ghosts are in attendance including Moaning Myrtle who haunts the first floor girl's bathroom. Later as they reenter the entrance hall, Harry hears the menacing voice (from the last chapter) call out again. Like before, he is the only one who can hear it. Harry chases the sound of the voice to the second floor where he finds Filch's cat, Mrs. Norris, hanging by her tail from the bracket of a torch, appearing to be very dead. On the wall beside her someone has written: "The Chamber of Secrets has been opened. Enemies of the Heir, Beware."

TUNIC (PAGE 123)

The kind of tunic that Nearly Headless Nick is wearing when he meets Harry in the hall is called a doublet (see *doublet*, the next definition). And since he is also sporting a ruff (see *ruff*), this means that Nick is dressed in an outfit popular during the Elizabethan era, or during the reign of Queen Elizabeth I (1558-1603).

The tunic, however, has been around since the times of ancient Greece and Rome. The basic tunic is a simple loose slip-on garment that is knee-length, sleeveless and worn with a belt. Made of linen or white wool, tunics were worn by both men and women, mostly as undergarments.

In the Middle Ages in Europe, tunics grew sleeves and were traditionally knee-length for men and full-length for women. Medieval knights wore them as well. Under their armor, they donned a kind of tunic called a gipon.

In the 14th century, a great movement called the Renaissance started in Italy. During this period, artists embraced classical ideals, among them the glorification of the human form. As the influence of the Renaissance spread throughout Europe, it had a definite impact on fashion. The old plain loose tunic was replaced with the fitted tunic which was mostly worn by men to show off their strapping physiques. This might have looked good on some of them but was probably a fashion disaster on the portly Middle Ager. This new tighter tunic evolved into what became known as the doublet.

DOUBLET (PAGE 123)
Doublets came into fashion in the early part of the 16th century and were famously worn by the big guy himself—England's King Henry VIII. They were padded garments decorated with jewels and embroidery that fit snugly around the male torso and were belted at the waist. The earliest doublets were knee-length and featured a gored or tapered skirt below the waist. Henry VIII and other well-dressed men of the era would wear a velvet gown over their doublet. This outer garment also came down to the knees and featured puffy sleeves which gathered above the elbow. To finish off the ensemble, every self-respecting 16th century male wore the must-have accessory of the time—hosery. Unlike modern panty hose that come to the waist, fitted hose for the doublet set were worn on each leg from foot to high-thigh. (Yes, we're still talking about men's fashion!)

As decades passed, the doublet lost its skirt and became an upper garment that could be buttoned or hooked closed in the front. By the end of the 16th century, the Elizabethan man wore his doublet with matching trunk hose (little puffy short pants that gathered at the waist and upper thigh), a Spanish style cape, a starched white ruff around his neck, and of course, a pair of hose (to cover his pasty white British legs).

Since Nearly Headless Nick is wearing a doublet and a ruff, I have assumed that he was an Elizabethan man (meaning he lived in the late 16th century). But we are soon to learn that Nick died nearly a hundred years before in the year of Christopher Columbus' voyage to the Americas (1492). Is Nick a fashion statement ahead of his time or did he just assume this dress style as a ghost? There is only one woman who can say for sure—and that woman is not me.

HUNT (PAGE 123)

Nick is ineligible to become a member of the "Headless Hunt" because his head is still somewhat attached to his Casper-like body. Since the Middle Ages, Huntsmen and Huntswomen in real-life British society were those who joined aristocratic hunting associations or 'hunts.' Mounted on horseback and accompanied by packs of hounds, they would pursue all variety of prey (deer, bear, boar, fox, etc.).

In the modern era, it was the fox that was hunted. Wearing black boots and riding attire (bright red tunics, white jodhpurs or riding pants and black hats), these huntspersons would gallop behind a pack of bloodthirsty hounds on the scent of a defenseless fox. Hunts took place over large open areas of countryside and if the fox was caught by the dogs, it suffered a terrible fate. Because of this, fox hunting was banned in Scotland in 2002 and then in England and Wales two years later. Traditional fox hunting is still legal however in Northern Ireland.

The late 19th century playwright and wit Oscar Wilde described this gruesome sport as "the unspeakable in pursuit of the uneatable." I'm with Oscar on this one.

POLO (PAGE 124)

We learn that one of the sports played by the members of the Headless Hunt is Head Polo. In the Muggle world, polo is an equestrian sport played between two teams consisting of four players each. But unlike Head Polo, they use a ball, not a head, to score their points.

The game is played on a field (not a pitch) with goal posts at each end. During four 7 1/2 minute periods called Chukkas, players use long-handled mallets to try and hit the ball through the opposing team's goal while on horseback. And like almost every other game in the world, whoever scores the most goals wins.

Although extremely popular in England, the game of polo did not originate there. It is the world's oldest equestrian sport and dates back to 6th century B.C.E. Persia (modern day Iran). British tea planters who lived in India took up the game in the mid-19th century where they established the Calcutta Polo Club. Shortly thereafter, polo moved to Great Britain and stayed.

Today, polo is played all over the world. It is a favorite sport of Prince William and Prince Harry.

TOPSHAM (PAGE 127)

The Kwikspell correspondence packet contains a glowing blurb from a woman in Topsham (pronounced Top-some). Topsham is a small town in Devon (remember that's the county in the southeast of England where Nicolas and Perenelle Flamel live). Near the city of Exeter, Topsham is a just short drive from the English Channel.

DIDSBURY (PAGE 127)

Another endorsement comes from a warlock who lives in Didsbury. This is a small village located in the northwest of England near the large industrial city of Manchester.

NUN (PAGE 132)

The "gloomy nuns" who show up at the Deathday Party were at some point living women who belonged to a monastic religious order. Remember when we talked about monks—the guys who live in monasteries and devote their lives to God. Well, Roman Catholic women who do the same are called nuns and often live in nunneries.

Holy women were part of religious orders as far back as the 4th century. Orders of nuns required their members to take vows of chastity, obedience and poverty, and much of their time was spent in reading and prayer. By the 16th century in Europe, many active orders were established where their members worked in communities as teachers or nurses. But it was also at this time that everything began to unravel for the nuns and monks of England. Here's the backstory:

The big guy, King Henry VIII, wanted to get a divorce from his first wife Catherine of Aragon (daughter of Ferdinand and Isabella of Spain) so he could marry his soon-to-be second wife, Anne Boleyn. But he had to get the pope's permission to do so because divorce was against the rules of the Catholic Church. Up until this time, England and all other Christian countries of Europe were loyal to the Roman Catholic Church and the pope who is the head of the Roman Catholic Church. So, in all matters religious, it was the pope who had the power. But this was changing—in large part due to the acts of a monk in Germany named Martin Luther who questioned the authority of the pope and the Church. The movement he started became known as the Reformation and was about to create sweeping changes throughout the continent.

So when the pope refused to grant Henry VIII a divorce, Henry decided to take matters into his own hands by perpetrating a little Reformation of his own. He broke off all ties with the Roman Catholic Church and set up his own Christian church called the Church of England. Since he was the head of this new church, Henry could okay his own divorce and marry the girl of his dreams. For Anne, the future queen, this turned out to be a most unfortunate turn of events because the king had her executed about three years later (see *beheading*).

So how does this have anything to do with the nuns of Britain? Plenty. Because the nuns were faithful to the pope, not Henry. In something that all British school children learn in history class as the 'Dissolution of the Monasteries,' nunneries and monasteries were abolished and their treasures seized by the crown. During Henry's reign, around 11,000 nuns and monks were forced to leave their communities and were given little or no money to do so. Needless to say, this was a very bad time for the orders of nuns and monks.

It wasn't until the 19th century that nunneries began to reappear in England, way too late for those who fell prey to the antics of King Henry VIII and the impact of the Reformation.

KNIGHT (PAGE 132)

When Harry and his mates see a knight at the Deathday Party, they are looking at a ghost who at some point in history was knighted by a king or queen of England. The tradition of knighthood originated in the Middle Ages of Europe as a way to honor brave cavalrymen (soldiers who rode on horseback).

In folklore, knights served King Arthur of Camelot and became part of the legendary Knights of the Round Table. A knight lived by the code of chivalry, a set of values that included bravery in battle and loyalty to king and country. They also saw themselves as the protectors of women. Over the centuries, the process of becoming a knight became formalized and often a boy would start his training for knighthood as early as the age of seven.

In the late 11th century, knights began journeying to the Middle East to fight in the Crusades, which turned out to be a number of ultimately unsuccessful campaigns to take the Holy Land from the Muslims. During this time, knights embraced Christian ideals and founded powerful knightly orders such as the Knights Templar and the Knights Hospitallers. Crusaders who were knighted at the tomb of Christ became known as Knights of the Holy Sepulchre.

By the 16th century, as the role of the knight warrior diminished in the face of more modernized warfare, knighthood became an honorary title that a king or queen could use as they saw fit to reward distinguished individuals—like government officials, military heroes and great artists.

The warrior tradition of dubbing a man into knighthood by touching him on the shoulders with the flat side of a sword remains today. In the present-day ceremony, the knight-to-be kneels before

Queen Elizabeth (or sometimes Prince Charles or Prince William) and she touches him on the shoulder with a blade of a sword.

Nowadays, knights can be women, too. Whereas a male knight is addressed as 'sir' (remember Sir Paul McCartney), his female counterpart is referred to as 'dame.' In the *Harry Potter* movies, the role of Professor McGonagall is portrayed by a woman who has been knighted for her contribution to the dramatic arts in the United Kingdom. She goes by the official moniker of Dame Maggie Smith.

HAGGIS (PAGE 133)

Now if this doesn't make you mouth water, I don't know what will. I am *so* kidding! Because haggis is an abomination (whether it is covered with maggots or not). Picture this: organ meat (heart, lungs, liver) from a calf or sheep mixed together with suet, onions, spices and oatmeal. This tantalizing concoction is stuffed into a sheep's stomach and boiled like a sausage to revolting perfection. It is then served with 'neeps' and 'tatties' (turnips and potatoes).

You might ask, who would eat such a thing? And I might answer, the Scots.

Haggis is a traditional Scottish dish that is a favorite on Burns' Night which is celebrated every January 25th in Scotland. This annual evening of feasting and merry-making honors the late national poet of Scotland, Robert Burns, who lived from 1759-1796. (Maybe he would have lived longer if he hadn't eaten so much haggis!) Alright, I'll stop with the haggis jokes. It's unfair. The Scots are lovely people, haggis might not be so bad after all, and I don't want Ewan McGregor to be mad at me.

HUNTING HORN (PAGE 135)

A hunting horn is a small simple instrument that is somewhat like a bugle but is curved in shape. During the hunt, a rider on horseback would blow the hunting horn to initiate the hunt. The horn could also be sounded to provide signals to the galloping huntsmen and women during the event.

At the Deathday Party, the hunting horn heralds the arrival of the "headless horsemen," as well as the utter mortification of Sir Nick.

LORDS (PAGE 136)

I must confess, I have been somewhat dreading this definition because, to me, the subject of the British nobility is complicated and strange. So bear with me as I attempt to give you the best explanation of it I can.

Here goes. The social structure of Britain was based on the class system which is a hierarchy based on one's standing in society. What this basically means is that if you were born into an aristocratic family, you would forever be an aristocrat. Conversely, if you were born to a poor family, you would probably forevermore be poor. The class system was a rigid thing that rarely allowed anyone to move beyond the 'class' into which they were born. Mostly, people knew their place (as awful as that sounds) and were resigned to remain there.

Because of this, many people who were not born into 'noble' families felt as if there was little chance of bettering their lives. That's why so many of them left the British Isles in the 17th and 18th centuries to come to the New World (aka America)—a place of opportunity where they could have a new start. Their resolve was so strong that they eventually fought a war against their king (George III) to gain independence from such a restrictive society. This, of course, was the Revolutionary War and was the beginning of our country as we know it today.

Now, this is not to say that there is no social hierarchy in this country, because of course, there is. But it's less restrictive and more covert. In the U.S., even a son of a president wants to be known as a common man.

But in Britain, the nobility or aristocratic class is well laid out and established. People of 'noble' birth often have titles to go along with their inherited lands and lifestyles. I explained this in brief under the definition of barons but now, we will take a closer look.

The term 'lord' comes from the Old English word 'hlaford' which literally means 'bread keeper.' It became a general and somewhat informal title for a nobleman who was a member of the 'peers of the realm.' This means that at some point in time, a king or queen gave that person a title and made him a lord. Once titled, he had the right to sit in the House of Lords which is one of the houses of Parliament. The other is called the House of Commons which consists of elected officials.

When a lord died, his oldest son inherited his title as well as his seat in Parliament. No other experience or acumen was required. These lucky firstborns were called 'hereditary peers' and have been passing down their titles and privileges from generation to generation ever since. Over time, hereditary peers eventually included some women.

Traditionally, the House of Lords (also called the House of Peers) has been broken down into two groups—the biggest and mightiest being the hereditary peers, also called the lords temporal. But the House of Lords also included archbishops and bishops who were known as the lords spiritual.

In 1958, Parliament established a thing called the 'life peerage.' This meant that the Prime Minister could bestow an honorary title of nobility to some person he or she thought worthy. The title granted to most life peers was that of the baron, the lowest titular rank of the peer of the realm. Life peerages were usually given to government officials, military officers and sometimes people in the arts and entertainment field. Because the honor only lasts for one's lifetime, the life peer could serve in the House of Lords but their offspring would not inherit their seats. (I told you this was going to be complicated.)

But being governed by people who were not elected, (i.e., the entire House of Lords) began to wrangle many Brits who were *not* to the manor born. Because of this, the House of Lords started to be reformed in 1999. Since then, many lords have lost their seats in Parliament as the British government started trying to figure out what the House of Lords should become. The House of Lords can still introduce and debate legislation but is restricted by the Parliaments Acts when it comes to rejecting bills passed in the House of Commons.

But long, long before there was any thought of reshuffling the House of Lords, the five orders of the peers of the realm were established. Definitely, a freaky concept to us because we don't have anything like it. In fact, until I started researching the titles themselves, I had no idea what the difference between them was. The closest I had come to nobility was in the movies when I would hear someone refer to someone as a Duke or a Countess. That was just some strange and exotic European thing that as an American, I didn't have to understand.

But I have come to believe that the more we know about other cultures, the better. Even if it is about this. So, without further ado, I give you the five orders of the peerage, starting with the highest of its ranks. The Duke.

1. Duke

The term duke comes from the Latin word 'dux' which means leader. The title of duke is mostly reserved for royalty although it does include some non-royals. Historically, a duke presided over his dukedom, which was a designated area of land in Britain.

The first dukedom was created in 1337 by King Edward III when he elevated his son, Edward the Black Prince, from the rank of Earl of Cornwall to that of Duke of Cornwall. (Remember, Cornwall is where the pixies live.) An example of the creation of a modern day dukedom occurred in 1947 when Queen Elizabeth II made her husband, Prince Philip, the Duke of Edinburgh. Prince William is the Duke of Cambridge and Prince Harry is the Duke of Sussex.

Unlike the other orders of the peerage, dukes are not informally called 'lords.' They are strictly referred to by their formal titles.

The female equivalent of a duke is called a duchess. Throughout history, most duchesses gained their titles the old fashioned way— by becoming Mrs. Duke. (Think Duchess Catherine and Duchess Meghan.)

2. Marquis (or Marquess)

Marquis (pronounced Mar-kwiss with the stress on the first syllable) comes from the old French word 'marchis' which means 'count of the marches' (in France, marquis is pronounced mar-kee). The title marquis ranks second to that of the duke.

The first marquis was Robert de Vere, the Earl of Oxford. Richard II created the title of Marquis of Dublin for him in 1385. The female equivalent of a marquis or the wife of a marquis was called a marchioness.

A nobleman who was a marquis would have been referred to informally as a lord. For instance, Robert de Vere's formal title was the Marquis of Dublin, however, he would have been less formally addressed as Lord Dublin. In the House of Lords, his peers would have simply called him Dublin.

This is an important note to keep in mind when reading about the lower ranking titles of nobility to come. Because when a noble's title (other than a duke's) is tied to that of a territory (e.g., the Marquis of Dublin), the prefix "lord" can be combined with that territory as an alternative to the noble's complete title (i.e., Lord Dublin).

In the case of the life peerage, the title of lord is combined with the person's surname. For example, when the renowned actor, Laurence Olivier, was granted the first life peerage to go to someone in the dramatic arts in 1970, he went from being Sir Laurence (as a knight) to Lord Olivier (as a baron). Stay with me, people!

3. Earl

The title earl is the oldest rank in British nobility and was introduced during the reign of the Danish king, Canute, when he ruled England from 1016 to 1035. The word is derived from the Danish 'jarl' and the old English 'eorl' which meant a 'man of position.'

It was the highest noble rank until the title of duke came along in 1337. Now, earl ranks a disgruntled number three, outdone by those sneaky marquises.

The title of earl was originally bestowed on important military administrators, many of whom gained political power. When William the Conqueror conquered England in 1066, he tried to change the title of earl to that of 'count' which had a more distinctive European flavor. But the title of count never caught on—except with the women. Because ironically, the wife of an earl is called a 'countess.'

4. Viscount

The viscount is number four in the aristocratic food chain, right under earl. The title of viscount (pronounced vie-count with the stress on the first syllable; the 's' is silent) comes from the old French word 'visconte' which means 'deputy of a count.' This makes a lot of sense now that we know a count is the European equivalent of an earl.

In Britain, the title of viscount was first bestowed on John, Lord Beaumont in 1440, although the rank had been around for centuries in other European countries like France and Spain. A female viscount (usually Mrs. Viscount) is called a viscountess.

5. Baron

The lowest rank of the peerage. As we learned earlier (back in the *Sorcerer's Stone* section), the word 'baron' came from old French and was imported to England when William the Conqueror invaded in 1066. At first, barons were servants of nobles or the king. By the 13th century, they were separated into the categories of lesser and greater barons which was largely determined by their land holdings. Over time they became nobles and were invited to sit in the House of Lords. A female baron (or wife of a baron) is referred to as a baroness.

So, there you have it! The five orders of the British peerage. It will be interesting to see how the powers of these hereditary aristocrats continue to change and evolve in the future.

A last little footnote. A hereditary peer can be granted more than one title. For instance, someone might be a duke as well as an earl. Let's look at Prince Charles of England (present day heir to the throne and dad of Princes William and Harry) as a great example of multi-titled madness. Not only is Prince Charles the Prince of Wales, he is also: the Duke of Cornwall, the Duke of Rothesay, the Earl of Carrick and the Baron of Renfew, among others. Seems like a lot of titles for a single prince. But as I've said before, we're

Americans and as such, the peerage will probably never make much sense to a bunch of 'commoners' like us!

LADIES (PAGE 136)

'Lady' comes from an Old English word which literally means 'bread kneader,' opposed to the Old English meaning of lord which is bread keeper. At first, the term simply referred to the lady of the house.

In the British peerage, 'lady' is a general title for a woman of noble rank less than that of a duchess. The courtesy title of lady is bestowed on daughters of dukes, marquises and earls. Also, wives of knights are referred to as ladies.

I would say this has been quite enough about the British nobility. If it hasn't given you a headache (it's given me plenty), feel free to move on to Chapter 9.

– CHAPTER 9 –
THE WRITING ON THE WALL

CHAPTER SUMMARY:
Filch accuses Harry of killing his cat but Dumbledore realizes that the cat is not dead, simply petrified. Dumbledore assures Filch that Harry would not have the ability to do such a thing and a potion made from the Mandrakes (when they mature) will be able to revive her. Hermione learns that the Chamber of Secrets is a chamber beneath the school built by Salazar Slytherin that can only be opened by his heir. When opened, a monster will be released to purge the school of Mudbloods. Harry, Ron and Hermione think that Draco Malfoy must be the Heir of Slytherin. They decide to make a Polyjuice Potion to change them temporarily into Slytherins to trick Malfoy into revealing the truth.

HELD BACK (PAGE 146)
When we hear that someone has been held back in school, it usually means that he or she has to repeat a grade. But in this chapter, when Harry is "held back in Potions," it doesn't mean he has to take the class again. Instead, he's required to stay after the regular course period and perform a nasty chore for Professor Snape.

MEDIEVAL (PAGE 147)
Looking back through this text, I see that I've used the word 'medieval' many times without a proper explanation of what it really was.

The medieval period is synonymous with the Middle Ages in Europe, which began around the time of the fall of the Roman Empire (the 5th century) and spanned nearly 1000 years. Almost everything that can be attributed to the Middle Ages can be described with the adjective medieval. You've got your medieval castles, your medieval knights and even your "Medieval Assembly of European Wizards." But as the Middle Ages petered out around the time of the Renaissance, all things medieval came with an expiration date.

STAFF ROOM (PAGE 148)
Teacher's lounge. That mysterious place where teachers go to escape their unruly charges.

SPOT (PAGE 156)
Harry, Ron and Hermione find Moaning Myrtle in the bathroom "picking a spot on her chin." This makes perfect sense if you're a Brit because a "spot" is what they call a pimple or a zit. Sad to think that even ghosts have to endure such ghastly things.

But there's another specifically British usage for spot that denotes a small amount. In this case, spot can be used somewhat ironically. For instance, when my husband takes a break in the afternoon for a spot of tea, I know for a fact that he's not going to stop at a mere sip.

THICK (PAGE 160)
Ron thinks that no teacher would be "thick" enough to help them check out the book from the library that contains the recipe for Polyjuice Potion. (Have they met Professor Lockhart?!)

If a Brit says, "How thick are you?" he or she is not asking how fat you are, but rather how stupid, dumb or dense you are. I don't know which is less flattering! 'Thick' is commonly used in the same way that we say 'dumb.'

– CHAPTER 10 –

THE ROGUE BLUDGER

/

CHAPTER SUMMARY:

With the help of the unsuspecting Professor Lockhart, Hermione acquires the ingredients for Polyjuice Potion. Meanwhile, Harry breaks his arm during a Quidditch match when he is attacked by a "rogue bludger." Lockhart performs a charm that accidentally removes the bones from Harry's arm instead of mending it. In the hospital wing, Harry receives a visit from Dobby who says he was behind the bludger incident to scare Harry away from Hogwarts because it's not save for him to remain there. Dobby flees when Dumbledore and Professor McGonagall enter the hospital wing carrying a petrified Colin Creevey.

TRANSYLVANIAN VILLAGER (PAGE 161)

Harry is forced to portray a Transylvanian villager in Professor Lockhart's class. If you'll recall from earlier, Transylvania is where Bram Stoker's fictional vampire (see *vampire*), Dracula, comes from. In his book, Transylvanian villagers were superstitious people who lived in fear of their blood-sucking neighbor. Although Dracula is a supposed fictional character, there is nothing fictional about the region of Transylvania. Surrounded by the Carpathian Mountains, the Transylvanian Alps and the Bihor Mountains, Transylvania is part of modern-day Romania.

TEA-STRAINER (PAGE 163)

If Professor Lockhart trapped a ghoul in a tea-strainer, that must have been a very small ghoul indeed. A tea strainer is a gadget (usually made of metal) with a handle that has a small wire-meshed cup on its end. When pouring tea from a teapot, you place the meshed part between the pot and your teacup. The tea strainer catches any bits of loose tea that come through the spout. It's an excellent invention if you drink tea the old fashioned way, brewing loose tea in a pot. No strainer required when using tea bags.

NATIONAL SQUAD (PAGE163)

The National Squad would be the national quidditch team—England's team—that would compete against other national teams in the Quidditch World Cup (see *World Cup*). Again, this is modeled on soccer where a professional player from a local team gets 'capped' for England which means he is asked to play on the national squad. It's something akin to our all-star teams where a great player joins a team of the other great players but also remains a member of his local team.

Professor Lockhart claims he was capped for the National Squad. I'll believe it if you do.

TODDLE UP (PAGE 173)

No-arm-bone Harry is told to "toddle up to the hospital wing" by Professor Lockhart who just rendered him boneless. This is a friendly yet patronizing way to tell someone to go somewhere, literally in the manner of a toddling baby. To 'toddle up' means to go up somewhere (so the hospital wing is either up a hill or upstairs). And 'toddle off' means to simply go off somewhere. I imagine it's hard for Harry to toddle up or toddle off anywhere in his present condition.

TIDY (PAGE 173)

Instead of saying that Madame Pomfrey can fix Harry's boneless arm, Lockhart says she can "tidy him up a bit." Of course, we know what 'tidy' means—to make something neat. But the Brits take this tidy business to a whole new level. To tidy yourself is the same as to smarten yourself, meaning to neaten yourself up or make yourself presentable. A British mother would be tidying up her child when she spits on her hand and wipes his or her face with it. Sadly, American mothers have been known to subject their children to similar treatment.

In this situation, Professor Lockhart is being a bit ironic because it is going to take more than tidying to re-grow the bones in Harry's arm.

TUT-TUTTING (PAGE 174)
Tut-tutting is like our tsk-tsking. Both are attempts at phoneticizing or spelling out that sound we make to express disapproval. They say 'tut-tut.' We say 'tsk-tsk.' But here, J.K. Rowling uses tut-tutting metaphorically. Instead of uttering the sound (tut-tut), Madame Pomfrey is lacing the words she speaks in a tone of disapproval.

WOOLLY (PAGE 179)
A woolly is what the British call a woolen jumper. Translation—a pullover sweater knitted in wool.

DRESSING GOWN (PAGE 179)
A robe. The kind you put on over your pajamas. In the past, such a robe would have often been called a dressing gown in this country but now, it seldom is. However, over there, a robe is *always* called a dressing gown. No exceptions.

So when Professor Dumbledore rushes into the hospital wing wearing a long woolly dressing gown, it tells us someone got him out of bed for important Hogwarts' business. As we soon discover, that's exactly what happened.

NIGHTCAP (PAGE 179)
With a nightcap on his head, Dumbledore must look like he's awoken from another time. Because even though Brits and Americans have been known to wear nightcaps to bed on cold winter nights, it's

rarely done nowadays. The traditional nightcap is long and woolen and is worn pulled down over the ears. My husband assumes that no one has actually worn one since 1897 (or thereabouts).

Chapter 11

The Dueling Club

Chapter Summary:

While Harry creates a diversion, Hermione steals the last two ingredients for the Polyjuice Potion from Snape's office. At the Dueling Club, Harry is paired with Malfoy who conjures up a long black snake that comes out of the end of his wand. When the snake goes after Justin Finch-Fletchley and Harry yells for it to stop, it becomes apparent that Harry is a Parselmouth—someone who can talk to snakes. It's a rare gift, and one that Salazar Slytherin possessed. Students begin to suspect that Harry might be the heir of Slytherin and matters only get worse when Harry is later caught standing alone over Justin's petrified body. Professor McGonagall marches Harry to Dumbledore's office.

At The Ready (page 191)

This is how we would say 'on your mark.' It's what Lockhart says to Harry and Malfoy right before they begin what's supposed to be a harmless duel. Or course, you can never trust a Malfoy and the duel turns out to be much more dangerous than expected.

Been Down For Eton (page 198)

We learn that Justin Finch-Fletchley had "been down for Eton." As stated earlier, that means Justin had been accepted to attend Eton, the exclusive Muggle school outside of London (see *Eton*). But unluckily for him (at least in this chapter), Justin chose Hogwarts instead.

BALACLAVA (PAGE 201)

In the hallway, Harry runs into Hagrid who's looking like some kind Arctic hunter, partially because he is wearing a balaclava. A balaclava is a woolen garment worn over the head and neck which covers the whole head except for the nose and eyes. Meant to keep the chill out, balaclavas were originally worn by soldiers on active duty in cold weather climates.

The name comes from the town of Balaclava (or Balakclava) in the Crimea, a peninsula in Eastern Europe located between the Black Sea and the Sea of Azov. The Crimean War (1854-1856) was a war between the Russians and the Turks. The Turks' allies in this war included England and France. During the Battle of Balakclava, the British sustained very high casualties and Alfred Lord Tennyson wrote about this ill-fated battle in his famous poem, *Charge of the Light Brigade.*

ROTTER (PAGE 203)

When Peeves calls Harry a "rotter" in song, it's an old fashioned way of saying that he's a no-good or bad fellow. My husband tells me it's an 'upper class' word of disapproval that would have been a staple among boys at places like Eton. For Harry, it's unfortunate that such a lousy word happens to rhyme with his last name.

– CHAPTER 12 –
THE POLYJUICE POTION

CHAPTER SUMMARY:

In Dumbledore's office, Harry is shocked when the headmaster's bird bursts into flames. After they watch the phoenix's rebirth from the ashes, Dumbledore tells Harry he believes in his innocence. By Christmas day, the Polyjuice Potion is ready and after the Christmas feast, Harry and Ron knock out Crabbe and Goyle with a sleeping potion, hide them in a closet, and take a hair from each of their heads to add to the potion. After Harry turns into Goyle and Ron becomes Crabbe, they find their way to the Slytherin common room and engage an unsuspecting Malfoy in conversation. To their surprise, they discover that Malfoy is not the heir of Slytherin after all and that he has no idea who is.

FAWKES (PAGE 207)

In the definition of Bonfire Night (see *Bonfire Night*), we learned all about Guy Fawkes and how he gets burned in effigy every year on November 5th. The difference between Professor Dumbledore's phoenix (see *phoenix*) named Fawkes and the real Guy Fawkes is that after the phoenix burns, he comes back to life again. Not so for the unfortunate man of the same name.

PLUM CAKE (PAGE 212)

The plum cake that Harry receives from Mrs. Weasley for Christmas would be a kind of fruitcake made with plums. I say yuck … but maybe Harry likes it.

CHOCOLATE CAKES (PAGE 213)

The chocolate cakes this year go to that dreadful duo, Crabbe and Goyle. Little do they know that these cakes—probably the size of Twinkies—were prepared by Hermione especially for them. Filled with "sleeping draught," they'll knock Malfoy's sidekicks out for hours. 'Draught' is how they spell our word 'draft.'

CHRISTMAS TEA (PAGE 214)

Remember 'tea' can be a way of describing a meal as well as a drink. In this case, tea refers to the Christmas dinner our pals have just enjoyed.

PUDDING BOWL HAIRCUT (PAGE 217)

When the Polyjuice potion turns Ron into Crabbe, we're told that the ever-fashionable Slytherin sports a 'pudding bowl haircut.' This would be the same as our 'bowl cut' but in the British version, it's a pudding bowl (a bowl in which one makes British pudding or dessert) that would be placed over the poor kid's head to cut the hair that's left hanging around it. Or we could just call it a very out-of-date hairstyle.

JUMPED UP (PAGE 223)

When Malfoy describes Hermione as a "jumped up Mudblood," it's not a compliment. What he's actually calling her is an uppity, social climbing peasant. To the class-conscious Malfoy, Hermione is someone pretending to be of a higher social class than she comes from. What an unmitigated snob!

DRAWING ROOM (PAGE 224)

In disguise, Harry and Ron learn about the Malfoy's father's Dark Arts chamber that's hidden underneath their drawing room floor. Originally, a drawing room was called a withdrawing room but the term was shortened in the 17th century. It was a parlor where guests could withdraw to after dinner and relax in a slightly less formal setting than the formal dining room. Old manor houses like the Malfoy's would definitely have such a room. Think of the board game, "Clue," which is set in a manor house. The solve of a particular murder could be: Miss Peacock, with the lead pipe, in the drawing room.

Nowadays, a drawing room is still the place in English homes to receive guests. Often called a sitting room or a lounge, it's the main room for entertaining guests in the house.

Ho! (PAGE 224)

An exclamation of surprise or victory. When Ron lets a "ho!" slip after hearing about the Malfoy's secret chamber, he's saying "Ah ha! Got ya, Draco!"

– CHAPTER 13 –
THE VERY SECRET DIARY

CHAPTER SUMMARY:
While Hermione is in the hospital wing due to an unpleasant reaction to the Polyjuice Potion, Harry and Ron return to Moaning Myrtle's bathroom where they find the blank diary of T. M. Riddle. Hermione suggests the diary might have hidden powers and an accidental encounter between Harry's ink bottle and a singing dwarf proves she was right. Harry discovers that when he writes in the diary, the ink disappears and is replaced with a reply. A boy named Tom Riddle who attended Hogwarts fifty years ago writes back to Harry through the diary. Riddle says that he caught the person who killed a student and opened the Chamber of Secrets fifty years ago. Magically, Tom reveals that the culprit was Hagrid.

SMARMIEST (PAGE 228)
'Smarmy' is a word that we might say from time to time, but Brits use it much more regularly. Ron calls Professor Lockhart the "smarmiest bloke" he's ever met. It doesn't take much to guess what he means—ingratiating, obsequious, too willing to please. All accurate descriptions of the oily Professor Lockhart.

SONNETS (PAGE 231)
A sonnet is a short poem that comes out of the Western European literary tradition. Having fourteen lines and a specific rhyme scheme, the sonnet is divided into two different categories: the Italian (or

Petrarchan) sonnet and the English (or Shakespearean) sonnet.

The sonnet was first introduced in Italy in the 13th century. It reached its highest expression with a poet named Petrarch (hence, the Petrarchan sonnet). He wrote over 300 sonnets for a woman named Laura that are some of the most beautiful love poems ever written.

When the sonnet came to England from Italy in the 16th century, the timing couldn't have been better. It was the Elizabethan era and the arts where flourishing there like never before. William Shakespeare (1564-1616), perhaps the greatest playwright and poet of all time, established the English sonnet as one of the primary poetic forms of the next four centuries.

The English or Shakespearean sonnet was all about rhyme and rhythm. Like the Italian sonnet, the English one was comprised of fourteen lines. The first eight lines (called the octave) set up a question or problem which was answered or resolved in the last six lines (called the sestet). But differences developed. The rhyme scheme of the English sonnet was altered to better suit the English language. Also, it incorporated the rhythm of iambic pentameter. This means that each line consisted of five stresses or beats.

Over time, the English sonnet took on themes such as religion and politics in the writings of poets like John Donne and Milton. But the love sonnet saw a revival in the 19th century with the works of poets like Elizabeth Barrett Browning and Dante Gabriel Rossetti.

Poetry was the dominant literary form for many centuries—way before anyone ever thought about writing a novel. And the sonnet is one of poetry's most beautiful inventions. So, check it out! Read a sonnet! And if that's not your cup of tea, you might as well try a ...

LIMERICKS (PAGE 231)

... limerick! Limericks are funny things, often in the literal sense. They are short little ditties, often nonsensical, composed of five lines with a defined rhyme and rhythm scheme. Their subject matter can range from the cute and clever to the brash and bawdy.

Though no one knows for sure where the limerick originated,

many believe it came from an Irish soldier's song from the 18th century called *Will You Come Up to Limerick?* (Limerick is a town in southern Ireland.) One of the earliest and most famous collections of limericks came from the English writer, Edward Lear, in his 1846 *Book of Nonsense*. By the early 20th century, the limerick was so popular that many magazines held limerick contests. People would send in their poems and hope to win. Here's my submission:

> *There once was a wizard named Potter,*
> *Who worked magic with quill and with blotter,*
> *No Muggle nor bum,*
> *A hero to some,*
> *But to Peeves he was always a rotter.*

Yes, it makes no sense and yes, it's awful. But hey, I didn't say it was going to be a good limerick. Just count yourself lucky I didn't try a sonnet!

BATH (PAGE 231)

A city in southwest England. Like the city of London, Bath (or Aquae Sulis as they originally called it) was founded by the Romans. They were attracted to the area because of its natural hot water springs indigenous to the region. The Romans fashioned the town after a Roman city and erected classical buildings and Roman baths. These hot baths would inspire the city's eventual name.

The Romans liked to be clean (good on them Romans) and were known for their elaborate bathhouses. These were large beautiful buildings designed for group bathing (men and women separate, of course). In 1755, one of these Roman baths was rediscovered in Bath and furthered the city's renown as a fashionable spa and resort destination. If you go to Bath today (and I highly recommend that you do), you can't help but see the stamp of Rome on this distinctly British city all these many centuries later.

VAUXHALL ROAD (PAGE 231)

T.M. Riddle's blank book that Harry and Ron find in the girl's bathroom came from a variety store on Vauxhall Road in London. Before we get to Vauxhall Road, let's take a moment to explore this variety store thing. Because frankly, I was a little confused by it. A variety store is an American term for a shop that sells lots of small items. It made me think of the Woolworth's of my childhood. Although today's version would be more like a 7-11.

I still needed clarity. What exactly was a British variety shop? So, I went to my secret stash of British edition Harry Potter books and turned to Chapter 13 in the *Chamber of Secrets*. In place of variety shop, I found the term 'newsagent,' and realized that American editors had made the switch. That's because a newsagent isn't exactly like a Woolworth's or a 7-11. They're more newsstand than convenience store. Selling mostly magazines, newspapers, a few paperbacks and maybe even a blank journal like the one Harry found, a newsagent would also carry, to a lesser degree, candy and little 7-11 type items. The newsagent is the convenience store of Britain. Good thing to know when you're visiting there and want to grab a quick Mars bar or a copy of *The Times of London*.

Now that that's settled, we can move on to Vauxhall Road. This would put our newsagent in the district of Vauxhall which is on the south bank of the River Thames in London. In the 17th century, this area became known for its public gardens and was a popular resort area. Unfortunately, the urban sprawl of the 19th century forced the close of the gardens, and they became a casualty to what the modern world calls progress.

– CHAPTER 14 –
CORNELIUS FUDGE

CHAPTER SUMMARY:

Harry's room is ransacked and Tom Riddle's diary is stolen. When Harry hears the menacing voice again, Hermione realizes what it might be and runs off to the library while Harry hurries to his Quidditch match. But the game is cancelled because two more students have been petrified—and one of them turns out to be Hermione. As the school goes under a kind of martial law, Harry and Ron use the invisibility cloak to sneak down to Hagrid's hut where Dumbledore, Cornelius Fudge and Lucius Malfoy show up. Fudge is there to take Hagrid to the wizard's prison (Azkaban) and Malfoy is delivering the Order of Suspension to Dumbledore. Hagrid's parting words to the invisible boys are: "Follow the spiders."

SCHOOL GOVERNORS (PAGE 261)

The 'school governors' is just the kind of group that could banish our Hagrid from Hogwarts. It's what we would think of as a school board at private schools. Unelected and ultimately powerful.

Yet the term 'governor' has other uses over there. A governor is a representative of the British government appointed to rule colonies and Commonwealth countries. At one time, these governors were literally stationed all over the world, when the sun never set on the British Empire. In the American colonies (before we kicked them out), our states were run by British governors. And we still call the heads of our states governors today.

In Britain, however, the word governor is not just reserved for heads of a region or state. An employer or a person of perceived social authority can also be called governor (often pronounced 'guvner' or simply 'guv') as a show of respect. Watch a British period drama on PBS or Netflix and you'll see what I mean.

– CHAPTER 15 –
ARAGOG

CHAPTER SUMMARY:

Harry and Ron follow the spiders deep into the Forbidden Forest. After finding Mr. Weasley's enchanted car, the boys are captured by giant spiders and carried to their leader, Aragog. They learn that Aragog was Hagrid's "monster" which people believed came from the Chamber of Secrets fifty years ago. But Aragog says this wasn't so—that the real monster still lives in the castle today. Although they barely get out of the spiders' den alive, Harry and Ron gain two important bits of information: Hagrid is not the heir of Slytherin and the girl killed fifty years ago died in a bathroom. Could that girl have been Moaning Myrtle?

CARTHORSES (PAGE 276)

The spiders in the Forbidden Forest are described as being a big as carthorses—or as big as horses that pull carts or wagons. We would more commonly call this kind of working animal a draft horse. But who cares what they're called when you find a bunch of spiders as big as that!

– CHAPTER 16 –
THE CHAMBER OF SECRETS

⚡

CHAPTER SUMMARY:

Harry and Ron pull a piece of paper from Hermione's petrified hand which tells them that the monster in the Chamber is a Basilisk—a giant snake whose stare is fatal. The voice of the basilisk is what Harry has been hearing. On their way to tell Professor McGonagall, the boys learn that the monster has taken Ron's sister, Ginny, into the Chamber of Secrets. Entering the Chamber through Moaning Myrtle's bathroom, the boys drag along a reluctant Professor Lockhart for help. In an underground tunnel, the cowardly Lockhart attempts to cast a Memory Charm on the boys which backfires. Part of the tunnel collapses, trapping Harry on the other side. Harry goes on and, by himself, enters the Chamber of Secrets.

BEDSIDE CABINET (PAGE 289)

The bedside cabinet next to Hermione's bed in the hospital wing is what we would call a bedside table that happens to have drawers.

– CHAPTER 17 –
THE HEIR OF SLYTHERIN

CHAPTER SUMMARY:
Inside the Chamber, Harry finds an unconscious Ginny and a seemingly alive Tom Riddle. We learn that Tom charmed Ginny through his diary into opening the Chamber of Secrets. The real shocker is that Tom Riddle is actually the teenaged Lord Voldemort. As Voldemort releases the basilisk, Fawkes (Dumbledore's phoenix) arrives in the Chamber carrying the Sorting Hat. While Harry tries to avoid the basilisk's deadly stare, Fawkes punctures the serpent's eyes, giving Harry a chance to pull a sword from the Sorting Hat and kill the serpent. When Harry stabs the diary with a basilisk's fangs, the young Voldemort disappears. Fawkes flies Harry, Ginny, Ron and Lockhart back to Moaning Myrtle's bathroom.

DREW LEVEL (PAGE 306)
Harry "drew level with the last pair of pillars" in the Chamber of Secrets. To draw level means to come even with something, in this case, the pillars. In sports, the British also use the term to describe the score when two teams have tied. Strangely, to us, a sportscaster there would never say that West Ham and Manchester United (U.K. football teams) tied. He or she would instead say they 'drew level' if the score was even during the game (once the game—or match—was over, they'd describe a tied game more simply as 'a draw').

– CHAPTER 18 –
DOBBY'S REWARD

CHAPTER SUMMARY:

As Harry explains what happened in Professor McGonagall's office, Lucius Malfoy barges in with Dobby in tow. Harry accuses the elder Malfoy of planting Tom Riddle's magic diary on Ginny at the bookstore at Diagon Alley at the beginning of the school year. Saying it can't be proved, Malfoy storms out of the office. Harry goes after him and hands Malfoy the diary, wrapped in one of Harry's dirty socks. When Malfoy angrily discards the sock, Dobby catches it, thus becoming free (that's what happens when a house-elf is given a piece of clothing by his master, even if by accident). Later, at the feast, Harry is congratulated and Gryffindor wins the House Cup for the second year in a row.

NO NEW ENTRIES. On to *Harry Potter and the Prisoner of Azkaban*!

- Part Three -

Harry Potter

AND THE

PRISONER OF AZKABAN

– CHAPTER 1 –
OWL POST

CHAPTER SUMMARY:
Harry is back at the Dursley's during the summer break. After a late night secret study session, he realizes he has just turned thirteen and owls arrive delivering presents from Ron, Hermione and Hagrid. Ron's birthday card comes from Egypt where he is vacationing with his family after winning the Daily Prophet Draw, which gave them enough money for the trip. An enclosed clipping from the Daily Prophet shows a photograph of the Weasley family including Ron's rat, Scabbers. The owls have also brought a letter from Hogwarts and a permission slip for the Dursleys to sign to allow Harry to visit the wizarding town of Hogsmeade during the school year. It's his happiest birthday ever.

WITCH BURNING (PAGE 1)

As Harry prepares his essay about "Witch Burning in the Fourteenth Century," he learns that real witches only pretended to be burned by the Muggles who occasionally caught them. I don't know if there were real witches back then but many people believed there were and those suspected of being witches were in mortal danger.

The practice of witchcraft has been written about since the times of ancient Greece and is mentioned several times in the Bible. The early Christian Church frowned upon the use of witchcraft, claiming that witches used their supernatural powers for evil purposes and were connected to Satan. Witches were accused of being heretics—a catchall word for anyone who didn't adhere to orthodox Christian doctrine. In 1231, Pope Gregory IX instituted the papal Inquisition to combat heresy. A convicted heretic who did not recant his or her views was often put to death. By the 15th century, things really heated up for a suspected witch, often literally. This was the time of the Spanish Inquisition when the Spanish Christian leadership gained the authority to go after heretics in particularly vicious ways. They burned heretics by the thousands, many of them alleged witches. The anti-witch fervor was further stoked in 1484 with the publication of the *Malleus Maleficarum* (*The Hammer of the Witches*). Written by two German Dominican friars, it became the authoritative text in Christian Europe on the evils of witchcraft and incited a three centuries long campaign against those who were suspected.

Among the things that Protestant settlers brought with them to the New World was their fear of witches, which reached a level of sheer hysteria in 1692 in New England culminating in the famous Salem witch trials.

HARRY'S YEAR (PAGE 5)

This simply means Harry's grade. The way we Americans refer to being in fourth grade, fifth grade, etc., Brits refer to being in Year Four, Year Five, and so on. Ron, Hermione, Neville and Malfoy are all in Harry's year. They will, for the most part, remain in the same group until they graduate—as long as everyone passes their exams, that is!

EGYPT (PAGE 8)

The lucky Weasleys have gone to Egypt for their summer vacation (or summer holidays, as they would say).

Egypt, a country located in the northeastern corner of Africa and home to one of the oldest continuous civilizations in the world, grew up around the River Nile (which happens to be the longest river on the planet, by the way). What we know of Ancient Egypt mostly comes from what has been found in their tombs. Historians divide this era into three periods: the Old, Middle and New King-doms. These kingdoms spanned over 3000 years until Alexander the Great invaded the country in 332 B.C.E. After the Greeks, Egypt was occupied for many years by the Romans (big surprise). In 642 C.E., Arabs gained control, making Egypt an Arabic-speaking and Muslim state and, in 1517, the Ottoman Turks invaded and began to rule the region.

And then the British stuck their noses in. Or at least tried. In the early nineteenth century, the British wanted to secure their trade routes through Egypt. They also wanted to rule the world. But so did France (more on this out-of-control rivalry coming up) and, to the dismay of Britain, Napoleon Bonaparte snatched Egypt from right under its fingers. But those Brits, as we know, are a tenacious lot and, shortly after their occupation of Egypt in 1882, the country became a Protectorate of Great Britain, a nice way of saying that the Egyptians were out of power and the Brits were in. But if history has taught us anything it's that no country likes to be occupied. Conflict and civil unrest gained Egypt a kind of nominal independence in 1922, but it took a military coup in 1952, and the ascent of the first native Egyptian ruler in over 2000 years, to send the British packing. The British attempted to regain control in 1956 by combining forces with the Israelis and the French and occupying the Suez Canal zone, but times had changed and Britain was no longer the superpower it once was. The new big kids on the block (the U.S. and the Soviet Union) pressured Britain and the others to get out. And they did, averting the Suez Canal crisis and leaving the rule of Egypt finally in the hands of the Egyptians.

PYRAMID (PAGE 9)

In the photograph in the *Daily Prophet*, the Weasleys are standing in front of a pyramid. What that means is they're standing in front of an ancient burial tomb.

A pyramid is a great monumental structure with a stone facing built with a rectangular base and four triangular sides sloping up to an apex. As incredible as the pyramids are on the outside, though, it's what was inside that really mattered: an interior chamber or tomb where a royal person, often a pharaoh (an Egyptian king), was laid to rest after he or she died. (Yes, there were some female pharaohs, including Nefertiti and Cleopatra.)

The Egyptian pyramids are very famous, especially the Pyramids of Giza that were built between 2530 and 2470 B.C.E. This cluster of three pyramids is the oldest of the Seven Wonders of the Ancient World and the only one that remains today. The oldest and tallest of the pyramids is called Cheops (at nearly 500 feet tall) and was named after King Khufu who reigned during its construction. Next to these pyramids stands the Great Sphinx, a stone carving with a body of a lion and royal head, which rises to 65 feet. The Pyramids of Giza are located on the Giza plateau near the city of Cairo and were considered the tallest structures made by humans until the Eiffel Tower was completed in 1889.

It was a British archeologist, Sir William Matthew Flinders Petrie, who was the first to excavate the site using modern techniques in the 1880s. He established the standard for how archeological excavations would be performed in Egypt when the British and others starting laying claim to these ancient tombs.

TOMBS (PAGE 9)

A tomb is a burial chamber, but the Egyptian tomb housed much more than a dead body. The ancient Egyptians believed in an afterlife and the contents of their tombs reflected this. The royal corpse was mummified (an elaborate process of preserving the body) and many of the dear departed's possessions and reminders of his mortal life were entombed with him. Great treasures, wall paintings of scenes from their lives, sculptures of loved ones—all these kinds of things made their way into the dead Egyptian's tomb. This way the spirit could enjoy his body and his things in the afterlife. At least that was the theory.

But what happened was this: These tombs, being filled with

incredible treasures, were just too much for some land-pirates to resist and it wasn't long before tomb-raiders were sneaking inside the pyramids and stealing all the treasure. This prompted the pharaohs to ditch the pyramid/tomb idea and come up with a safer alternative.

Enter the Valley of the Kings. Located in Thebes, this valley became the preferred burial site for pharaohs (and some queens) beginning with King Thutmosis (reigned 1506-1493 B.C.E.). The young king was the first to build his burial site there. In all, about sixty royal tombs were buried deep into the mountains surrounding the valley. It was a good idea and a valiant effort. But it didn't stop the raiders. They got into those tombs as well. Well, at least into most of them.

Then came the modern tomb raider, and our British connection, Howard Carter. Carter was an archeologist (one who studies ancient people by excavating their civilizations) and Egyptologist (an archeologist who specializes in Egyptian old stuff). In 1922, Carter uncovered one of the most celebrated discoveries of the 20th century in the Valley of the Kings—the ancient royal tomb of Tutankhamen, pharaoh of Egypt from 1333-1323 B.C.E. Miraculously, the tomb was still intact and its contents undisturbed. That is, until Carter disturbed them. Carter and his associate, Lord Carnarvon, oversaw the excavation of King Tut's tomb and what they found was amazing. It was full of treasures including the solid gold coffin which housed the mummified body of Tutankhamen himself. When Lord Carnarvon died during the excavation, and his dog died at the very same time back in England, people began to talk and the legend of the Curse of Tutankhamen was born. Was it just a coincidence or was some ancient curse at work in the death of this modern day grave robber? Guess only Carnarvon and his dead dog know for sure.

SEVENTH YEAR (PAGE 10)
The final year! A seventh year student (age 17-18) is in his or her seventh year of secondary school, equivalent to our twelfth grade.

The coming school year will be the last one for Ron's brother, Percy.

FEZ (PAGE 10)

In the picture of the Weasleys in Egypt, Percy is wearing a fez. A fez is a hat that was often worn by Muslim men, and that would include most Egyptian men. The fact that Percy is wearing such a hat tells us that if he were visiting France, he would probably don a Frenchman's beret, and in Norway he might put on a Viking hat with horns. By wearing a fez on their vacation, Percy is showing himself to be an enthusiastic tourist. So good for Percy. He's actually having some fun for a change.

A fez is shaped like a cut-off cone. It's made of red felt with a flat top that sports a tassel. Its name comes from the city of Fes in Morocco where the fez was manufactured exclusively until the late 19th century.

Today, some people wear fezzes in Britain and in this country, perhaps most notably the Shriners—a Masonic organization whose members wear their red fezzes to Shriner events and meetings. But there's another group in the U.K. whose members wear fezzes—the Laurel and Hardy Fan Club. Laurel and Hardy were very famous film comedians who began in the silent movie days and continued into the early 1950s, and the official name of their fan club is The Sons of the Desert (named after one of the duo's movies). Oliver Hardy was an American but Stan Laurel was an Englishman and together, they were dead funny. In recent years, Matt Smith of *Doctor Who* (the famous BBC program about the Doctor who travels through space and time in his Tardis) was known to wear a fez.

FRANCE (PAGE 11)

France is a country in Western Europe that lies across the English Channel from Britain and, of all the countries in all the world, it's with the French that the British have the most entangled and complicated of histories. They have been the worst of enemies (they fought a Hundred Years War, for heaven's sakes) and occasionally the closest of friends (World Wars I and II come to mind). Each has, at times, conquered and ruled the other and—despite the official pacts of friendship and cooperation signed in 1904 and known collectively as *L'Entente Cordiale*—that rivalry is never far below the surface. The French contempt for British cuisine and couture is matched only by the British contempt for the French's sad condition of Not Being British.

PERMISSION FORM (PAGE 14)
You know, that thing you have to get your parent or guardian to sign in order to go on a school field trip. Aka, a permission slip.

– CHAPTER 2 –
AUNT MARGE'S BIG MISTAKE
O─O

CHAPTER SUMMARY:

The next morning, Harry and the Dursleys see pictures of an escaped convict named Black on television. Then Harry's mood turns black when he learns that Aunt Marge is arriving and staying for a week. A deal is struck: if Harry will keep his mouth shut about his wizarding life, Uncle Vernon will sign his permission slip for Hogsmeade. But when Aunt Marge belittles Harry's parents, Harry finally snaps. The Dursleys watch in horror as Aunt Marge magically expands and is lifted off her chair to the ceiling. After brandishing his wand at Uncle Vernon, Harry leaves the house with his trunk, books and Hedwig's cage and finds himself alone in the darkness of Privet Drive.

LAYABOUT (PAGE 17)

When Uncle Vernon sees the picture of the wild-looking prisoner named Black on the television, he calls him a "filthy layabout." A layabout is someone who is a habitual idler, loafer or general lazy no-account. The word started being used in the mid-20th century, probably by people as intolerant as dear old Uncle V.

RUNNER BEANS (PAGE 17)

The runner beans in the Dursleys' next door neighbor's garden can be one of several types of beans that grow in vine-like stems and are twined around wooden posts or stakes to keep them supported.

Where I come from (in the southern U.S.), we call them pole beans.

MUSICAL STATUES (PAGE 18)

Aunt Marge has had a long history of being nasty to Harry. In fact, on Dudley's fifth birthday, she hit Harry with her stick so he'd lose against Dudley at musical statues. Huh? What are musical statues? Statues that play musical instruments? No, it's a kids' game like musical chairs only instead of rushing to find a seat when the music stops, you rush to freeze in place. Whoever takes longest to stop moving is kicked out until only one player is left and declared the winner. Just so you know, the British play musical chairs, too—and, apparently, we in the U.S. also play musical statues, except we call it The Freeze Dance.

RIPPER (PAGE 18)

Not only does Aunt Marge terrorize Harry, her little dog does, too. And what a name for a terrorizing dog! Here's a brief history lesson about a terrible man with the same name.

It happened over a hundred years ago in London's East End, a traditionally working-class area that is the home of 'Cockney Rhyming Slang' (more on that in the next chapter). In 1888, a man terrorized the East End neighborhood of Whitechapel for four months, murdering seven women. It was a gruesome affair (way too gruesome to deal with in this book) causing a public uproar in and beyond the East End. In a letter he sent to the newspapers the killer called himself Jack the Ripper and, though the police made extensive efforts to capture him, they never did and the mystery of Jack the Ripper's real identity was never solved. Many movies have been made and books written on the subject and to this day there is much speculation and conjecture as to who he really was.

COLLECT (PAGE 18)

Uncle Vernon has words with Harry before going to "collect" Aunt Marge at the train station. For a moment I entertained the fanciful thought that he was going to add Aunt Marge to his collection of mean and nasty Dursley relatives. But, of course, that would be silly. Actually, Brits use the word "collect" to describe going to pick someone up from somewhere, whether a school, airport or train station.

SMART (PAGE 19)
When Aunt Petunia says that Dudley has to "make himself smart" for Aunt Marge, she could be asking of him the near-impossible. Because if "smart" means brains, poor Dudders is out of luck. But luckily for Dudley, Petunia just wants him to spruce himself up and look sharp and handsome for his aunt's arrival. Come to think of it, maybe she's asking the near-impossible after all.

CAR COAT (PAGE 20)
A car coat in summer! What is Uncle Vernon thinking? Truth is, the United Kingdom is known for its occasional wet and miserably cold summer day. One reason my husband found his way to sunny California.

A car coat is a short coat made especially for—can you guess—people who drive cars. Which I assume can be worn any time of year.

TWENTY-POUND NOTE (PAGE 22)
Like the ten-pound note that we learned about in Book Two, the British twenty-pound note is U.K. paper* currency. Like all other notes, the front of the twenty-pound note displays the likeness of Queen Elizabeth II (or whoever the current monarch is) while the back has an image of a notable person from British history (like Adam Smith).

*These notes will be made in polymer (like the current ten-pound note) in 2020. I just held my first polymer note—the material is a strong, thin plastic which will surely last much longer than paper money. Wonder when our greenbacks will follow suit?!

THRASHING (PAGE 24)
A "good thrashing" is what we would call a good beating, which is something Aunt Marge believes in heartily for bad kids like Harry and the others at his—or any—school.

NOSH (PAGE 27)
We think of a "nosh" as a snack between meals. But when Aunt Marge complements Petunia on the "excellent nosh," she's raving about a meal, not a snack. If it had been a very large meal, Marge could have called it a "nosh-up."

FRY-UP (PAGE 27)
A fry-up is exactly what it sounds like. Food fried up in a frying pan. You can have a fry-up at any meal in the U.K. Throw some bacon, eggs, mushrooms and tomatoes into a frying pan for breakfast—that's a fry-up. Throw some liver (yuck), onions and tomatoes into a frying pan for dinner—another fry-up. But who can tell what Aunt Marge would throw in a frying pan for a fry-up? If she had her way, she'd probably include Harry!

TWEED (PAGE 27)
Tweed is a woolen fabric that is flecked with color and is used to make clothes, often jackets. The manufacturing of tweed began in Scotland and it was originally known as "tweel" until an 1826 case of bad penmanship changed its name forever. Here's what happened: a shipment of tweel was delivered to London with a sloppily written shipping notice. The English recipients of the tweel thought that the notice read tweed. That coupled with the fact that the tweel manufacturer was based near the River Tweed in Scotland resulted in the name change. Tweel was out, and tweed was in. This should be a lesson to all of us with sloppy handwriting!

WASTREL (P. 28)
When Aunt Marge calls Harry's father a wastrel, it makes

Harry's blood boil. That makes perfect sense when you know that "wastrel" comes from the word "waste" and describes someone who is a spendthrift or a worthless, inferior layabout. Not a nice word to call somebody's father.

In Cornwall, in the southwest of England, a wastrel can also denote a strip of waste land or ground, usually along the side of a road.

– CHAPTER 3 –
THE KNIGHT BUS

⚡

CHAPTER SUMMARY:

In darkness, Harry walks to Magnolia Crescent where he encounters a huge dog-like creature which disappears into the night as the Knight Bus arrives. This triple-decker magical bus picks up "stranded" wizards and witches. On board, Harry learns that the escaped convict from the TV news is really a wizard (and supposed follower of Lord Voldemort) named Sirius Black who killed thirteen Muggles twelve years ago. Black is the first prisoner ever to escape from the wizard prison, Azkaban. Harry is dropped off at the Leaky Cauldron and met by Minister of Magic, Cornelius Fudge, who deposits him in room number 11 where Harry will be staying until the start of the school year.

MAGNOLIA CRESCENT (PAGE 31)

After leaving the Dursleys' house, Harry "collapses onto a low wall in Magnolia Crescent." Magnolia Crescent is a road. It could have been called Magnolia Avenue, Magnolia Lane or Magnolia Street but because this street is named Magnolia Crescent, it tells us something specific about it. In the U.K., a street that curves is traditionally called a crescent—think of the curve of a crescent moon, for instance.

There's another curious element to the above quotation. What about that low wall "in" Magnolia Crescent? Sounds a bit strange, right? That's because the British will sometimes say "in" instead of "on" when it comes to something positioned on or to the side of a street. We, on the other hand, would nearly always say that the low wall was "on" Magnolia Crescent.

PEBBLE-DASHED WALLS (PAGE 33)
The house Harry finds himself looking at on Magnolia Crescent has pebble-dashed walls. This means that a mixture of concrete and tiny pebbles has been applied over the brickwork or other existing exterior of the house. Pebble-dashing was quite popular in the 1950's and 60's but is rather out of fashion today.

TRIPLE-DECKER BUS (PAGE 33)
A triple-decker bus is a bus with three levels, which would make the Knight Bus a very tall bus, indeed. Certainly, the inspiration for the Knight Bus comes from the British double-decker bus—the red London double-decker being the classic and most famous. The double-decker buses that my husband rode in Liverpool when growing up were green through, and other cities have other colors. The classic double decker, whatever the color, had an open rear platform where riders could jump on and off (just like the Knight Bus does), but because that was deemed too dangerous in our 21st century world, the classic double decker model was phased out in 2005. Nowadays, those old red classic buses are mostly reserved for tourists who get to ride in style on their sightseeing jaunts around London.

THE KNIGHT BUS (PAGE 33)
The Knight Bus is a pun on the real Night Buses that run in London and other British metropolises. After the regular buses stop running (around midnight, depending on the city), Night Buses offer limited service on selected routes for the late night traveler. Although Harry's Knight Bus doesn't run exclusively at night, it does save stranded wizards—perhaps like a knight who'd rescue a damsel in distress.

BUS CONDUCTOR (PAGE 33)

Like American buses, most British buses are driver operated, which means you pay your money or show your pass to the driver when you get on board. But in the old days, drivers were sealed off in a cab or compartment in the front of the bus (to concentrate on driving) and a second employee, known as the conductor, dealt with the passengers in the bus. The conductor would walk up and down the aisles of both decks, collecting money and issuing tickets. This is why it was possible for passengers to board from the back of the bus. Because instead of paying the driver up front, the conductor would get their money once they were seated. The conductor would also ring a bell to let the driver know when to stop and when to start.

In days past, a female conductor was called a conductress but my husband fondly recalls calling such a woman a 'bus girl' when he was a little boy. He was so in love with this concept that he gave the name 'bus girl' to his favorite teddy bear. How sweet is that?!

COCKNEY ACCENT (PAGE 33)

This is Stan Shunpike's accent. To us, Stan the Knight Bus conductor sounds very strange but to the people of the East End of London (the mostly working-class boroughs to the east of the city), he sounds perfectly normal. Because Stan is what you would call an East Ender or a Cockney. A 'true Cockney' is said to have been born within the sounds of Bow Bells, which were the beautiful church bells that rang for hundreds of years at St. Mary-le-Bow. During World War II, when much of the East End was devastated in the German Blitz, the bells were sadly destroyed.

The Cockney accent is characterized by many things, most notably its rhyming slang and the dropping of h's. Rhyming slang can be extremely puzzling to the American tourist because it sounds like a kind of code—which in fact, it is. When I first went to London, I couldn't understand a word of it. Let me give you an example and you'll see what I mean. Upon seeing Hagrid, Stan might say, "Look at the great plates on that bloke." Huh? Is Hagrid wearing huge dinner plates on his head? No! Here's what a Cockney would hear: "Look at the big feet on that fellow." Still confused? I was, too, until I learned the trick to rhyming slang. See, most rhyming slang comes from compound words or phrases where the actual rhyming word is dropped. Okay, I know that makes no sense but read on.

In our example, 'plates' comes from the phrase 'plates of meat.' And meat rhymes with feet. But to confuse everyone else in the world, the Cockneys drop the rhyming word, in this case meat, and use the one that doesn't rhyme, in this case plates, to mean feet. Therefore, if you don't know the complete phrase from which the rhyming slang is derived, you have no way of knowing what they're talking about.

Here are more examples of rhyming slang: 'Stairs' are called 'apples,' from apples and pears. Pears rhymes with stairs but they use the word apples. 'Boots' are called 'daisies,' from daisy roots. Roots rhymes with boots but they use the world daisies. And the list goes on and on. My brother-in-law, Mike, who's originally from Liverpool, has picked up lots of Cockney slang since he's lived near London. And because of that he calls me a septic. Can you figure out what that means? I'm a Yank (what Brits call Americans) and what does yank rhyme with? Tank! So, he's actually calling me is a septic tank! (As you can see, I married into a most loving of families!)

Although Stan doesn't employ rhyming slang on the Knight Bus, he sure gives us plenty of other evidence of his Cockney origins. We'll start with his constant dropping of h's in words like Harry ('Arry), head ('ead), here ('ere), hand ('and), hot ('ot), have ('ave), her ('er) he ('e), who ('oo), his ('is), heart ('eart), heard ('eard), had ('ad), half ('alf), horrible ('orrible), hole ('ole), happened ('appened), has ('as), how ('ow), hear ('ear), him ('im) and hold ('old). Whew! I think I got all of them. Dropping your h's is a surefire way to sound Cockney. Try to say this: *At 'ogwarts, 'arry often 'as a cup of tea with 'agrid in 'is 'ut.* Get the picture?

Dropping the aitches is just the tip of this Cockney iceberg, though. The way Stan pronounces lots of words gives us more clues to his Cockney roots. Here, in order of appearance in this chapter, are some of Stan's words translated for you and me:

'Choo — what you?
Woss — what's
Nuffink — nothing
Dincha — didn't you?
Firteen — thirteen
An' — and
Toofbrush — toothbrush
Don' — don't
Fing — thing
Inee — isn't he?
Dinnit — didn't it?
Woz — was
Wiv — with
Anyfink — anything
'Cos — because
Din' — didn't
Didja — did you

Are you starting to notice some trends? Like the th sound becoming an f or a v sound. Or the t's-followed-by-y's becoming ch. Or the d's and t's and s's being dropped all together. That's Cockney for you.

One last note. Seeing these words in writing and being able to understand them when spoken by a Cockney are two very different things. The truth of the matter is this, when you travel to England and visit the East End, expect to understand nothing.

HEADLAMPS (PAGE 34)

We Americans would never refer to the lights at the front of cars or buses as headlamps—so it follows that Brits would never refer to them as headlights. But this is not true. It turns out that the terms are interchangeable in the U.K. and in fact, the use of 'headlights' is more common than 'headlamps.' Headlamps, like so many words and phrases in the Harry Potter books, is the more old-fashioned of the two, so therefore, the more desirable term in J.K. Rowling's world.

BOWLING ALONG (PAGE 35)
To "bowl along" means to move at a fast and smooth pace. In this case, the Knight Bus is bowling along some street in Wales.

WALES (PAGE 36)
Wales, like England, Scotland, and Northern Ireland, is one of the countries that make up the United Kingdom. Like England and Scotland (but unlike Northern Ireland), Wales is part of the U.K. mainland. Like Scotland and Ireland, Wales's political and historical relationship with England has been long and complex and not always friendly: conquests, independence, unifications, etc. The Welsh language, as a true native tongue, was all but lost by the beginning of the twentieth century but conscious efforts to reintroduce it into schools and onto road-signs have kept it alive. Wales has produced many well-known* writers, musicians, and actors—such as Dylan Thomas, Arthur Machen, Shirley Bassey, Tom Jones, Richard Burton, and Anthony Hopkins—and, since 2005, the global TV phenomenon *Doctor Who* has been produced in the BBC's studios in Cardiff, the Welsh capital. *Doctor Who* was first made in 1963 and many actors have portrayed the Doctor over the years, one of the most popular being David Tennant—who was also part of the cast of the Harry Potter movies. Who did he play? That's your homework for today.

*Well, well-known to your parents or grandparents, maybe.

BEST (PAGE 36)
This is a British colloquial form of 'better' when used as an imperative. We say, for example, "you better do that" and, though the Brits would say that too, they might alternatively say "you best do that," replacing 'better' with its superlative, 'best.' So when Ernie

tells Stan, "Best go wake up Madam Marsh," the driver is telling the conductor that he better go ahead and wake the witch up.

Note: If you're like me, this might not be an unfamiliar usage to you. My southern grandfather used this form of 'best' all the time.

ABERGAVENNY (PAGE 36)

Next stop on the Knight Bus, Abergavenny. This is a town in the southeast of Wales that is sometimes called the Gateway to Wales. Located at the head of a valley pass between the Brecon Beacons and the Black Mountains, Abergavenny has served as a strategic location since the Romans occupied Britain. The Romans built a fortress there and later, in the 11th century, the Normans (after William the Conqueror's conquest) erected a castle. Basically, it became a spot where conquerors guarded against the possibility of other conquerors. Today, all are welcome as Abergavenny is a tourist destination.

PRIME MINISTER (PAGE 37)

The prime minister is the head of the British Government. Unlike our president who is personally elected to run the government, the prime minister comes to power when his or her party wins a majority in the general elections.

Let me explain: There are two main parties in the British Parliament—the Conservative or Tory party and the Labor or Socialist Party. Members of Parliament (M.P.s) usually belong to one of these parties, although there are M.P.s from other parties as well. After a general election, whichever party has garnered the most votes will seat the most M.P.s in Parliament. (If you've been paying attention throughout this book, you know that these elected officials are the ones who will be sitting in the House of Commons.) Whatever party gets the most votes becomes the majority party. In our Congress, the majority party in each house has a majority leader. This is the same in the British Parliament but the majority party's leader becomes Prime Minister. Like our President, the Prime Minister is the head of government. Unlike our President, the Prime Minister is not the Head of State—that title, albeit primarily symbolic these days, is reserved for the current monarch (King or Queen).

Unlike our system where a president can be of one party and the Congress can be predominantly from another, their majority of members in Parliament and their prime minister always belong to the same party.

Some famous prime ministers include William Gladstone, Benjamin Disraeli, Lord Palmerston, Winston Churchill, Margaret Thatcher and Tony Blair.

FANCY HIS CHANCES (PAGE 40)
When Stan says "I don't fancy his chances," he is basically saying "I wouldn't bet on him" or "I don't think he has much of a chance." We've talked before about the various vernacular uses of 'fancy' in Brit-speak, and here it means something like 'having a favorable opinion of' (or, in this case, not).

THERE'S A GOOD LAD (PAGE 40)
Although the phrasing 'there's a' suggests something that is happening or has already happened, idiomatically this is actually a request: Ern is asking Stan to do him a favor, to do the right thing, which in this case is to change the subject and shut up about Azkaban. The use of 'a good lad'—because it sounds like something an adult would say to a child or teenager—might suggest Ern is older than Stan, but that's not necessarily true; contemporaries will happily say 'be a good lad' or 'there's a good lad' to each other in the U.K. when they're asking a pal to do something for them.

COLLYWOBBLES (PAGE 40)
Ernie doesn't like Stan talking about the guards at Azkaban. In fact, mere talk of the dreaded creatures makes him nervous and apprehensive, which in Ern speech means they give him the collywobbles. Derived from the words 'colic' and 'wobble,' collywobbles

literally means a rumbling in the belly or a stomachache—something the Azkaban guards (as we will later learn) have the ability to provoke with ease.

TELEPHONE BOOTHS (PAGE 41)
The British red phone booth (called a telephone box or kiosk) is a utility icon. They are beautiful to look at and once you've made a phone call from one, you'll be spoiled for other telephone booths forevermore.

Screech...Rewind...Who makes a phone call in a phone booth anymore? Okay, not many people. But these gorgeous red booths are classically British, just like the red double decker buses of days past in London.

Designed by Sir Giles Gilbert Scott, these booths used to dot the streets of the United Kingdom. Like the old public telephone booths in the U.S. (anyone remember them?), the British telephone box is completely enclosed with a door on one side. But unlike our old phone booths which were rather drab, the telephone box is bright red with lots of little paned glass windows. They are quite charming and very striking on the side of the street. However, in recent years, most of these telephone boxes have been done away with and replaced with more modern models. Sometimes progress really stinks! But luckily, a few remain for sentimental or historical interest. And sometimes they show up outside a pub or a hotel (even here in the USA!) to pump up the charm factor.

ANGLESEA (PAGE 41)
Wizards, as we learn from the books, seem to have a preference for old-school things—which perhaps explains this use of an archaic spelling for Anglesey, which is an island off the north coast of Wales connected to the mainland by the Menai Bridge. The seventh largest island in Britain, its current population is about 70,000 and humans have lived there since prehistoric times—as several megalithic monuments attest. Historically, Anglesey has long been associated

with the ancient Druid religion and was once known in Old Welsh as Ynys Dywyll, 'The Dark Isle.' Invaded and conquered over the centuries by Romans, Irish pirates, Vikings, and finally Edward I of England, it became a British county in 1284.

ABERDEEN (PAGE 41)
It's no wonder Harry's hot chocolate is spilled when the Knight Bus moves 'abruptly' from Anglesea to Aberdeen, because that's quite a jump; all the way from the coast of Wales to the northeast of Scotland. Aberdeen is the third most populous Scottish city and the educational center of its northeast region. Aberdeen University has been around since 1495—a good 200 years after it became a city under Royal charter from King David I of Scotland. Aberdeen has what is called a 'marine climate,' which translates to chilly summers. Let me assure you, if a Scotsman calls something chilly, any visiting Yank better wrap up real warm!

RIGHTO (PAGE 41)
Obviously a slangy extension of 'Right,' 'Righto' is basically a way of saying 'Okay.' Older Brits may employ variants like 'Right you are' or 'Righty-o,' though these are used a lot less these days.

CHARING CROSS ROAD (PAGE 41)
Despite the presence of the Leaky Cauldron and the entrance to Diagon Alley, Charing Cross Road is a real street in central London which for over a century was famous as the home of numerous anti-quarian and second-hand bookstores (or book shops, as you should call them if you ever shop there). Sadly, rent increases this century have forced many of the stores to close, though several remain.

PARLOR (PAGE 43)
In context, Fudge is talking about a private or semi-private room within a pub or hotel or restaurant, but 'parlor' is also used—at least by older generations of Brits—to mean a living room in a regular

house. It stems etymologically from the French verb 'Parler' (meaning 'to talk'), so the parlor is a place where you can have a good natter* with your mates. Or, in this case, an unwelcome natter with the Minister of Magic.

*Oh. Sorry. Have we not done 'natter'? Talk. Chat. Gossip. Chew the fat. Shoot the breeze.

NIGHTSHIRT (PAGE 43)
Once upon a time, everyone—men, women, grownups, kids, Brits, Yanks—wore nightshirts to sleep in. Then someone invented pajamas (or pyjamas, to the Brits) and the nightshirt went the way of the night-cap and the chamber-pot. Despite the 'shirt' bit, the nightshirt was a full-length and long-sleeved garment that wrapped you from neck to ankles and theoretically kept you warm while you slept in a world without central heating. Brrr.

– CHAPTER 4 –
THE LEAKY CAULDRON

CHAPTER SUMMARY:

While staying at the Leaky Cauldron, Harry spends time in Diagon Alley where he gets his first glimpse of the Firebolt, the newest thing in racing broomsticks. On the last day of summer break, Ron and Hermione show up (along with the rest of Ron's family). At the Magical Menagerie, Ron buys a tonic for his sick rat, Scabbers, and Hermione purchases a big ginger cat named Crookshanks. That night, at the Leaky Cauldron, Harry overhears Mr. and Mrs. Weasley saying that they think Sirius Black escaped from Azkaban to kill Harry and that Azkaban guards will be stationed around Hogwarts to try to keep Black from getting in.

OLD BOY (PAGE 50)

In the same way that blue-collar or middle-class Brits might refer to one another as 'mate'—"Can you give us a lift to the match, mate?" or "Fancy a pint, mate?"—their more upper-crust countrymen will use 'old boy.' Or at least they would have until sometime in the late 20th century. If said today, it's most likely to be used in an ironic (or at least knowingly old-fashioned) way. There's also something called 'the Old Boy network' which refers to the unspoken code in which people who went to the same posh high schools—even if not at the same time—will help each other out in later professional life. It's possible that 'old boy' as an affectionate form of address within the upper classes originates from this, though people don't have to have gone to the *same* posh school to use it with each other. An old Etonian (a man who went to Eton) will happily call an old Harrovian (a man who went to Harrow) 'old boy' without losing too much sleep over it.

IRISH INTERNATIONAL SIDE (PAGE 51)

The Brits often use 'side' to mean 'team,' so when the owner of Quality Quidditch Supplies tells the crowd that there's been an order for Firebolt broomsticks from the Irish International Side, he's just referring to the Irish quidditch team. The team is 'international' because they represent the entire country and play against other countries' teams in international competitions (like the World Cup) as opposed to the city or town based teams (often called clubs) that play against each other during the regular season.

WORLD CUP (PAGE 51)

When he refers to 'the World Cup', the proprietor of Quality Quidditch Supplies is talking about the Quidditch World Cup but the real-life model to which the QWC is analogous is the World Cup of the game that everyone else in the world calls 'football' and we Americans call 'soccer.'

Soccer is the most popular sport in the world and every four years the national teams from the countries who are part of FIFA (*Federation Internationale de Football Association*) take part in a knock-out tournament called the World Cup, first held in 1930. Thirty-two countries compete (after a long qualifying phase that includes many more), but as of this writing only eight countries have ever won the trophy: England and Spain (one win each), Argentina, France and Uruguay (two wins each), Germany and Italy (four wins each), and Brazil, which has won an impressive five times. Muggle enthusiasm for the sport (on both domestic and international fronts) is absolutely massive and seems to be matched in the wizarding world only by the fervent devotion to Quidditch by borderline-obsessive fans like a certain Ronald Weasley.

DIVINATION (PAGE 52)

Divination—or forecasting the future by one or other means of divine guidance or help—is certainly not uniquely British, being a part of many an ancient culture's way of life. But the Brits have surely been part of the long tradition of divination. And it's definitely a big part of the Witchy and Wizarding world of Harry Potter, as evidenced by the various sub-categories we learn that Harry will be studying this year at Hogwarts. We'll talk about these sub-categories after a quick diversion about paving.

PAVING SLABS (PAGE 52)

Used metaphorically here (to suggest how huge and heavy some of the spell-books are), paving slabs are technically larger than paving stones (see *paving stones*) but the truth is that, in casual conversation, Brits will pretty much use the terms interchangeably (not that I imagine slabs or stones come up that often in casual conversation, but you know what I mean).

CASSANDRA (PAGE 53)

Cassandra is the perfect name for someone who wrote a book called *Unfogging the Future*. Because Cassandra is a character in Greek literature who could do exactly that. The daughter of King Priam, the king of the ancient city of Troy, Cassandra was given the gift of prophecy (the ability to tell the future) by the Greek god, Apollo. However, when she angered the god, Apollo sought to vex her. He didn't take away her gift though. Instead, Cassandra retained her ability to foretell the future but Apollo made it so that no one would believe anything she foretold. Can you imagine her frustration? When her brother Paris brought the beautiful Helen back to Troy, she told him that their city would be destroyed. No one believed her. Then the Greeks came for Helen and began the Trojan War. And when the Greek's massive wooden horse was dragged through the gates of Troy and Cassandra said it was full of Greek warriors, nobody believed her. All I can say is they should have. Because Troy was sacked and poor Cassandra was taken back to Greece by Agamemnon, the commander of the Greek army, never to see her family or home again. And it gets worse. She dies. Murdered, in fact, by Clytemnestra, the wife of Agamemnon. But don't think it was a happy homecoming for Agamemnon. Because Clytemnestra killed him, too. It's a sad story with a sad ending. For poor Cassandra it could have all been different if only someone had believed her.

PALMISTRY (PAGE 53)

Palmistry is a form of divination. It is also known as chiromancy. 'Mancy' is a suffix that refers to seeing the future, and 'chiro' comes from the Greek word for hands. So, palmistry is about telling the future by palm reading. It's an ancient practice and is known to have been around in lost cultures like Babylon and Sumeria as well as nations that survive to this day like India, China, Egypt, and Persia (now known as Iran). The Greeks and Romans were interested in it too, including such notables as Aristotle and Alexander the Great. In medieval and renaissance Europe it was vigorously suppressed by the Catholic Church but enjoyed a revival—particularly in Britain—in the second half of the nineteenth century.

CRYSTAL BALLS (PAGE 53)

Crystal ball reading or crystallomancy—there's that 'mancy' suffix again—is the art of foreseeing the future through a glass ball. It dates back to at least the Druids of pre-Roman Britain and was championed in the reign of Elizabeth I by her court astronomer and alchemist, Dr. John Dee. Like palmistry, it too enjoyed a populist revival in Victorian times.

BIRD ENTRAILS (PAGE 53)

Hepatomancy, to give the reading of animal entrails its proper name, is—as you've probably already concluded—one of the grosser ways of foreseeing the future. Originally the -mancy of choice for the Ancient Etruscans, entrail-reading was also a big fave of the Romans and continued its ridiculous popularity deep into medieval times. It's asserted by some historians that even Thomas Beckett, an Archbishop of Canterbury, had a quick read of the guts before helping the Crown launch a military expedition against Brittany.

ARITHMANCY (PAGE 57)
Related to the wider-ranging occult discipline of numerology, arithmancy is—as you may have guessed from that familiar math-class prefix 'arith'—divination through numbers. No wonder it's one of Hermione's favorites.

RUNES (PAGE 57)
Though they have long been associated with magic and mysticism, the truth is that runes are simply letters that predate Europe's adoption of the Latin alphabet and were a means of writing down the words of ancient tongues like Old Norse or Anglo-Saxon. Or at least, that's what we've always been told. But if Hermione's studying a magic manual on ancient runes, then who can say for sure…

BANG HIM (PAGE 58)
Inside the Magical Menagerie, when Ron tells the witch about the ailing Scabbers and she says to "bang him on the counter," she doesn't mean that Ron should literally slam the poor rodent down on it. She's just telling Ron to place him there. She could just as easily have said "toss him on the counter" or "sling him on the counter." Or 'thow him,' or 'fling him.' Those Brits are so colorful.

WOEBEGONE (PAGE 59)
Scabbers is said to look woebegone compared to the other rats at the Magical Menagerie. While technically part of American English too, woebegone is hardly a word in everyday use here. 'Woe' means sadness or grief and 'begone' means … well, it doesn't mean 'begone' for a start. Instead it's the past participle of the obsolete

verb 'bego' and means 'surrounded by' or 'beset by.' So Scabbers is 'surrounded by sadness' or 'beset by grief.' But not really. As we know, the Brits will often use a word in a much lighter sense than its literal meaning implies. What's meant here is more along the lines of Scabbers looking tatty and unkempt. So we shouldn't feel *too* sorry for the little rat—which is good, considering what we learn later in the book…

TUTTED (PAGE 59)
We learned earlier that the Brits' tut-tutting is like our tsk-tsking. Both are attempts at phoneticizing or spelling out that sound we make to express disapproval. But here, J.K. Rowling uses tut-tutting metaphorically. Instead of making the actual tut-tut sound, Madame Pomfrey is lacing the words she speaks in a tone of disapproval.

SPIFFING (PAGE 62)
A Victorian and Edwardian era upper-class slang word meaning excellent or first-rate. If used at all now, it's mainly to mock upper class speech—or the pretensions of middle-class people who aspire to sound posher than they are. Which is exactly what George and Fred are doing here to their brother Percy. The first clue is that 'old boy' at the end of Fred's greeting to Harry, followed by George driving the point home with his "absolutely spiffing."

CORKING (PAGE 62)
Even after Mrs. Weasley tells the twins to stop their teasing, Fred gets one more jab in with his use of 'corking.' Like 'spiffing,' it's an outmoded piece of public-school slang meaning splendid or terrific.

CHOCOLATE PUDDING (PAGE 63)
We might think, for a brief ridiculous moment, that the Weasleys, Harry, and Hermione are being served the gelatinous goop* that we Americans call chocolate pudding, but I think we've learned enough about the British approach to desserts to know better, haven't we?

What's being dished up at the Leaky Cauldron is almost certainly another variant of the Great British Steam Pudding (see *pudding*), this time with added chocolate!

*perfectly delicious gelatinous goop, I hasten to add.

– CHAPTER 5 –
THE DEMENTOR

CHAPTER SUMMARY:

After boarding the Hogwarts Express, Harry, Ron and Hermione find a compartment all but empty, except for a sleeping man whose suitcase reads the name, Professor R.L. Lupin. When the train stops, a Dementor—a creature wearing a black cloak and hood—enters their compartment. Everyone goes cold, but Harry is affected most. He hears the sound of a woman screaming, then passes out. Professor Lupin casts a spell which causes the Dementor to retreat. At Hogwarts, Professor Dumbledore warns the students about the Dementors who are guards from the wizards' prison Azkaban. They will be guarding the school grounds and looking for Sirius Black. He also announces that Professor Lupin will be the new Defense Against the Dark Arts teacher and Hagrid will teach the Care of Magical Creatures course.

HERMES (page 70)

In Greek mythology, Hermes is the messenger of the gods and the conductor of the dead to Hades (the afterlife). He's also known for being a trickster, sometimes in the aid of humankind. The son of Zeus and the Pleiad Maia, Hermes is often represented wearing winged sandals and a winged cap. In Roman mythology, he is known as Mercury. We know that Percy Weasley is a bit of a scholar, so it shouldn't surprise us that he named his screech owl Hermes—a great name for an owl who delivers messages, don't you think?

INTERCITY 125 (PAGE 71)

This diesel powered, high speed, passenger train built by Muggles would surely grab the attention of Mr. Weasley on the King's Cross platform. It's called an InterCity because these trains were built for fast service between cities without those pesky stops to slow them down. The InterCity 125 came out in 1975 and its top speed—you guessed it—125mph. That's a fast train! Developed to modernize train travel in the U.K. and to compete with the expanding system of expressways (called motorways there), it broke world records in transporting passengers at high speeds. But time marches on, and the once modern InterCity 125 is being phased out for more modern passenger trains.

NUTTER (PAGE 75)

A nutcase or a crazy person. In British slang, nutter can be used playfully (to describe a friend who did something mental) or seriously (to describe someone who's out of their mind). In this case, Ron is clearly thinking that Sirius Black belongs in the 'out of his mind' category.

SWEETSHOP (PAGE 77)

Honeydukes is a sweetshop. Although J.K. Rowling conjured up Honeydukes, she did not invent the sweetshop. A sweetshop in the United Kingdom is what we would call a candy or confectionery store. These shops sell candy of course but nowadays most carry convenience store items as well. Traditionally, the British sweetshop would sell mostly boiled sweets, which are hard candies like humbugs. The oldest sweetshop in England is located in the village of Pateley Bridge in North Yorkshire and was established in 1827. I wonder how long Honeydukes has been around?

CHOCOBALLS (PAGE 77)

Pretty much like it sounds. Balls of chocolate. They can come in different sizes, with fillings or without. It sounds like the Chocoballs that Ron is salivating over must be pretty big to accommodate both strawberry mousse *and* clotted cream.

CLOTTED CREAM (PAGE 77)

Not only for Chocoballs! If you've been reading carefully, you already know what clotted cream is from the definition of 'tea' way back in Book One. But let's dig a little deeper, shall we?

Clotted Cream is an essential part of afternoon tea, a ritual that started in the 19th century where aristocrats had a fancy snack between lunch and late dinner. That snack would include things like tea, scones, crumpets, strawberry jam and of course, clotted cream. Clotted cream is a thick cream that comes from cow's milk. After it's heated, the cooling process creates 'clots' (sometimes called 'clouts') that form the cream. I know 'clots' might not sound particularly appetizing, but let me assure you there's nothing unappetizing about clotted cream. It's delicious. And super rich. And delicious. And extremely calorific. And did I say delicious.

Mostly made in the southeast of England in the counties of Devon and Cornwall, clotted cream is served on scones with jam. These counties have a tradition of doing this in their own ways though. In Cornwall, jam is spread onto the scone first and then the clotted cream is spooned on top. In Devon, the clotted cream comes first and the jam is dolloped on top. Weird, right? Can one method possibly taste different than the other? I guess we'd have to talk to the good people of Devon and Cornwall to know for sure.

LAMPS (PAGE 81)

If you're reading this book, chances are you've seen the Harry Potter movies, so you know what train cars on the Hogwarts Express look like—narrow corridors on one side only with doors leading into private(ish) compartments through the length of the car. Most U.K. trains looked like this all through the 19th and most of the 20th centuries (as did most U.S. trains), but I'm sorry to tell you that that's no longer true. Trains now, just like here, are mainly compartment-less open-plan row-seating cars and J.K. Rowling is being deliberately nostalgic and atmospheric in having the Hogwarts Express look so old-school. Which brings us, finally, to the use of the word 'lamps' when the carriage is plunged into darkness. Back when Sherlock Holmes and Dr. Watson were riding in the compartments of steam-driven trains, said compartments would be lit by gas lamps. Although electric lights were introduced on trains many many decades ago, the Brits still referred to them as 'lamps' rather than 'lights' right up to the 1960s or even '70s.

TURRETS AND TOWERS (PAGE 87)
On the stagecoach to Hogwarts, Hermione looks at the "turrets and towers" of the castle in the distance. FYI, turrets and towers are parts of medieval castles but they aren't the same things. Towers—which originated as military fortifications to keep enemies out—are circular structures, usually very large and fortified, that start at ground level and rise high from there. Turrets, also round but smaller and not starting at ground level, are usually situated on an angle or corner of a castle and project up from a higher level. These days, and certainly at Hogwarts, turrets with their pointed roofs are more for decoration than defense. At least, until we get to the later books!

SHOVE OFF (PAGE 88)
It's pretty self-explanatory, isn't it? Ron is telling Malfoy to leave in a not so friendly way. But believe me, the Brits have lots of even less friendly ways to tell people to move elsewhere, most of which I can't print here ('sod off' and 'sling your hook' are some of the milder variants). Shove off is essentially our 'get lost.'

FORTUNA MAJOR (PAGE 94)
The password at Gryffindor Tower is Fortuna Major. Which sounds pretty cool, and may be even more cool than you might think. Fortuna Major is the name of one of the main symbols in a

method of divination. Remember divination and all those '-mancies' from the previous chapter? Well, this branch of future-foreseeing is called geomancy, and once again its practice can be traced back to at least the Middle Ages in both Britain and the rest of Europe and to more ancient eras in Africa. 'Geo'—as in geography and geology—tells us that this time our medium for divination is the earth itself. Or at least bits of it. Practitioners interpret symbols formed from throwing rocks or dirt onto the ground and have a basic catalog of sixteen pre-determined geomantic figures that they can attempt to spot in the mess they've just made on a client's carpet. 'Fortuna Major'—which is Latin for 'the greater fortune'—is one of the sixteen geomantic figures and is said to illustrate good fortune growing from the earth and flowering or fruiting in the air and is therefore representative of power and success. By the way, all sixteen of the geomantic figures have names and some of them may sound just a little familiar to you: Cauda Draconis, Rubeus and Albus. Ringing any bells?

– CHAPTER 6 –
TALONS AND TEA LEAVES

CHAPTER SUMMARY:

Harry, Ron and Hermione receive their new course schedules and Ron questions why Hermione has so many classes—some even scheduled at the same time. In Divination Class, they meet their professor Sibyll Trelawney who claims to tell the future. She reads Harry's tea leaves and sees a Grim in them, a black dog which is a death omen. In the Care of Magical Creatures Class, Hagrid introduces the students to dangerous looking, half horse/half eagle creatures called Hippogriffs which he warns must be treated with the upmost respect. Harry has a successful interaction with the one called Buckbeak but when Malfoy disrespects Buckbeak, Malfoy lands in the hospital wing and Hagrid is sure he'll be fired.

PERCHANCE (PAGE 100)

As Harry, Ron and Hermione get lost on their way to Divination Class in the North Tower, Harry gets sidetracked looking at a "squat knight in a suit of armor" in one of the paintings. The indignant Sir Cadogan talks in what we could call knight-speak—the kind of talk we've come to expect from the mouths of knights and ladies in medieval times (even if, as any linguistic scholar will tell us, *actual* medieval people would speak a form of Middle-English that we'd hardly understand at all. Go check out Chaucer's *Canterbury Tales* in the original if you don't believe me). Sir Cadogan asks if our gang is making fun of him "perchance." He just means 'perhaps.' The two words were interchangeable and equally common in Brit-speak for many centuries and some affected Brits (or those mocking their affected brethren) will still use 'perchance' today. Etymologically, they're both compound words that have become diminutives over time. 'Per' is from the Latin and means 'by' and chance means chance (duh), while 'haps' is short for 'happenstance.' So, just like 'perhaps' means 'by happenstance,' so does 'perchance' mean 'by chance' (or, idiomatically, 'by any chance').

KNAVES (page 100)

This is what Sir Cadogan calls Harry, Ron, and Hermione when challenging them to produce their weapons. Now, if Sir C was a few centuries older, he might simply be being descriptive—because in Old English *cnafa* (the word from which knave was derived) merely meant 'boy' or 'child.' But, being the Medieval fellow he is, Sir Cadogan is in fact being derogatory and insulting, because by the Middle Ages, knave had come to mean someone untrustworthy and underhanded or (even worse!) someone of lower-class origins. The Jacks in packs of playing cards were for many years also referred to as knaves (Knave of Hearts, Knave of Spades, etc.).

SCABBARD (PAGE 100)

A scabbard is a sword (or knife) holder, sometimes made of leather, sometimes of metal.

SCURVY BRAGGART (PAGE 100)

Some more name calling by our less-than-friendly knight. 'Braggart,' as you can probably guess, is someone who brags or boasts a lot, but the adjective 'scurvy' is a little more antique. As a noun, scurvy refers to a disease caused by vitamin C deficiency and which was horribly prevalent in the 17th century among sailors on long missions at sea. Astonishingly, up to fifty percent of some crews could die of the disease. Only after a Royal Navy surgeon, James Lind, proved that citrus fruit could prevent the disease did

British ships set sail with huge stocks of lemons and limes. The use of the latter, by the way, is what led to Yanks calling Brits 'Limeys.'

CRINOLINES (PAGE 101)
When the knight bursts into a painting with women wearing crinolines he's doing a bit of time traveling because knights in armor do not belong in the same time period as women in crinolines. Crinolines—structured petticoats of horsehair and cotton that hold out skirts—did not become fashionable until the middle of the 19th century.

MENTAL (PAGE 101)
This is what Ron calls the knight after they've parted. Mental, strictly speaking, is a non-judgmental adjective pertaining to the mind. It could be good or bad, depending on context. Hermione, for example, could very often be praised for showing great mental dexterity while an unfortunate victim of a stupefaction spell could be said to demonstrate mental deficiency (hopefully temporary). It's a sad fact of Brit-slang that calling someone 'a mental case' has been a favored insult for nearly a century and, over the last few decades, the simpler 'mental' has been just as popular. What Ron is saying is that he thinks Sir Cadogan is mad (not mad as in angry, but mad as in insane).

SYBILL (PAGE 101)
Professor Trelawney's first name. It's an apt choice of name for a professor of Divination because it comes from the Greek word *Sibylla*, meaning Prophetess. It became popular as a first name in the Middle Ages and started being used in Britain after the Norman conquest (though usually spelled with just a single 'l'). Benjamin Disraeli, one of Queen Victoria's Prime Ministers, wrote a novel called *Sibyl* which helped the name come back into fashion in England in the second half of the 19th century, while Prunella Scales' performance as the mildly terrifying Sybil Fawlty in the 1970s BBC sitcom *Fawlty*

Towers helped send it tumbling back into disfavor in the second half of the twentieth.

TEA SHOP (PAGE 102)

Professor Trelawney's classroom is part attic, part tea shop. We've talked a lot about tea in this book but what about a tea shop? We have tea shops in this country, and they're mostly modeled on the British style: a small café/restaurant that, like a French patisserie, specializes *not* in full meals like breakfast, lunch, or dinner but in pastries, cakes, small sandwiches, scones, and of course ... Tea! Served properly in a pot and with fine china cups and saucers. J. K. Rowling is also, if we're honest, suggesting in the gentlest way that, like the lady herself, Sybill Trelawney's room is perhaps a bit, frumpy, old-fashioned, and chintzy.

POUFS (PAGE 102)

We'd probably call the things that some of the kids sit on in Professor Trelawney's room 'ottomans' and sometimes, so will the Brits. But more commonly those soft air or foam filled backless, legless, and armless chairs that can either be sat on or used as a foot-rest in front of a more regular chair are called Poufs, from the French, meaning something puffed out.

TEA LEAVES (PAGE 103)

Professor Trelawny does a pretty good job explaining how to prepare the tea leaves for reading so I won't dwell on that part. Just remember, she's talking about loose tea that has been poured in the teacup with the tea. At the end, the tea leaves or the dregs remain at the bottom of the cup. That's what a reader of tea leaves reads.

But what does it mean to read tea leaves? And how long has this been going on? Like all Divination, reading tea leaves is about foreseeing someone's future, like Trelawny does when she sees a Grim in Harry's teacup. The dregs of tea leaves make shapes that can be interpreted by people who know how to read those kinds of things. Reading tea leaves (along with reading wine sediments and coffee grounds) goes under the umbrella of a kind of divination called tasseomancy which literally means divination (-mancy) through the cup (tasse, the French word for cup).

WOOLLY (PAGE 111)

When Hermione accuses Divination of being 'woolly,' she's speaking metaphorically. Literally, a 'woolly' in Brit-speak is a wool sweater or cardigan. Metaphorically, perhaps because of the softness and fuzziness of wool, it means something that's imprecise, specious, or not-thought-through. It's a way to dismiss something as being silly or illogical.

SHARPISH (PAGE 115)

When Hagrid says "sharpish," he means to move away from Buckbeak quickly. Sharpish, like related words or phrases such as 'sharply' or 'look sharp' is a catch-all instructing people to pay attention, to concentrate closely, to move quickly, or any combination of the above!

WANTS A GO (PAGE 117)

This is like 'have a go.' When Hagrid asks if anyone else 'wants a go' at making friends with Buckbeak, he means does anyone else want to try it. If I were Malfoy, I'd think twice about wanting a go with the Hippogriff.

STEAK AND KIDNEY PUDDING (PAGE 119)

Remember earlier when I said that 'pudding' is the word they use in the U.K. to mean dessert? Remember when I also explained that it's a specific *kind* of dessert? Well...that wasn't exactly the whole story. But sometimes I think it's best to dole these things out in easy to digest morsels because clumped all together, they could cause brain damage. As well as being a synonym for any kind of dessert, as well as being various types of steamed sponge puddings, 'pudding' can also be used for certain types of savory pies. Strictly speaking, it should only be used when the pastry of the pie is made with suet as opposed to a more regular short-crust or flaky pastry but the truth is many Brits—particularly older ones, these days—will use pie and pudding interchangeably.

That's the pudding part. What about the steak and kidney? Well, inside that heavy suet full-case pastry you'll find, should you be foolish enough to look, a mélange of vegetables (mainly potatoes) in a thick paste-like gravy accompanied by free floating lumps of steak and, you guessed it, kidney.

TANKARD (PAGE 120)

The distraught Hagrid has clearly been drinking. A lot. And we're not talking lemonade. He drinks out of a tall (and here, bucket-sized) beer mug made of pewter called a tankard. Tankards often have hinged lids and sometimes have glass bottoms and although they are still seen decoratively in consciously old fashioned pubs and taverns in Britain, they've not been in common use for over a century now.

– CHAPTER 7 –
THE BOGGART IN THE WARDROBE

CHAPTER SUMMARY:

In double potions class, Seamus lets out that Sirius Black has been sighted in the Hogwarts area. Malfoy goads Harry to seek him out for revenge but Harry doesn't understand what he's talking about. Later, in the Defense Against the Dark Arts class, Professor Lupin teaches them how to defend against a boggart—a shape-shifter that takes the form of what you fear the most. To render the boggart harmless, you must perform a charm that makes it look ridiculous and makes you laugh. Neville successfully turns the boggart into the form of Professor Snape dressed in his grandmother's clothes. At Harry's turn, Lupin passes him over making Harry wonder if Lupin thinks he is up to the challenge.

TATTY (PAGE 130)

This is the condition of Professor Lupin's briefcase. Since 'tatty' means shabby, worn, or frayed, it could be time for Lupin to retire this briefcase and get a new one. Originating in 16th century Scotland, the Old English word 'taettec' means a rag or a tatter. 'Tatty' is a word my English husband says—especially about clothes. If I'm wearing a shirt that's seen better days, he might tactfully point out, "You might not want to wear that in public. It's a bit tatty." Which means, like with Lupin's suitcase, it might be time to ditch that shirt.

– CHAPTER 8 –
FLIGHT OF THE FAT LADY

CHAPTER SUMMARY:

It's October and Gryffindor Quidditch Captain Oliver Wood assembles his team and stresses his desire for them to win the Quidditch Cup this year. On Halloween, Harry (who doesn't have a signed permission slip) is left behind while other third year students visit the village of Hogsmeade. He wanders the corridors and ends up having a cup of tea with Professor Lupin in his office. Yet Harry becomes suspicious when Professor Snape shows up with a potion for Lupin to drink to help him feel better. After the Halloween feast, students from Gryffindor House discover that the portrait leading into their tower has been slashed and the Fat Lady who resides there has disappeared. Peeves tells Dumbledore the culprit was Sirius Black.

SPANKING GOOD (PAGE 144)

When Fred Weasley refers to Oliver Wood as a "spanking good Keeper," he means that Oliver is excellent at his job. In the U.S., spanking is mostly used literally, though occasionally we'll hear it as an adverb, as in 'spanking clean.' This latter usage is akin to the British one used here where 'spanking' is an adverb of degree—and means very or extremely. The earliest metaphorical use was nearly always used to qualify new (as in 'spanking new') and meant that something was as new as a newborn baby. How come? Because babies used to be almost automatically spanked by a doctor, nurse, or midwife immediately upon their arrival in the world. Not as a punishment, I hasten to add, but because it was thought to help 'get the system going.'

LOOKING DAGGERS (PAGE 149)

This is how Ron and Hermione look at each other when Professor McGonagall interrupts their argument. Think of it as mutual glaring, as if their eyes where throwing daggers at each other. Two thirteen year olds giving each other the stink eye. It's interesting how much Ron and Hermione's bickering accelerates in this book. What in the world could have them so bothered?!

BUTTERBEER (PAGE 158)

Now, let's be clear: 'Butterbeer,' as in the popular drink of the wizarding world, was made up by J.K. Rowling. But some—possibly reliable—internet sites say that at around the time of Queen Elizabeth I there was a beer that was made with butter, nutmeg, cloves, sugar and eggs. That "buttered beer" of over four hundred years ago was surely alcoholic (made in the days when beer was safer to drink than water in London) but I certainly hope that the butterbeer in Hogsmeade is a non-alcoholic brew if Ron and Hermione are drinking it.

YOUR HEADSHIP (PAGE 161)

When Peeves calls Dumbledore 'your Headship' he's not only being a creepy suck-up, he's being an inept creepy suck-up. Because there's no such word as 'Headship.' Peeves is trying, consciously or un-, to make an analogy with such actual formulations as 'your Lordship.' But in the time-honored tradition of verbally-incompetent-but-snobby lower-class servants in British comedy, he's quietly making a fool of himself.

– Chapter 9 –

GRIM DEFEAT

CHAPTER SUMMARY:

After the Fat Lady incident, all students at Hogwarts are required to sleep in the Great Hall that night while the professors search the premises for Sirius Black. He is never found. Days later, Harry is surprised to find Snape teaching Lupin's Defense Against the Dark Arts class. Snape gives them an assignment on werewolves. During the rainy Quidditch match between Gryffindor and Hufflepuff, Harry spots a big black dog high in the stands. When he feels cold, and hears a woman's screams, he looks down at the pitch to see dementors pointing up at him. Harry blacks out and awakens in the hospital wing, having fallen from his broom. Not only has his broomstick been destroyed, but Gryffindor lost the match to Hufflepuff.

ARGYLLSHIRE (PAGE 165)

Harry overhears that the Fat Lady has gone to hide in a map of this place. That means she's hanging out in a map of the county of Argyll, which is located in western Scotland. This part of Scotland stretches out into the sea creating islands in the north Irish Sea. To me, these islands vaguely look like teardrops about to fall on Northern Ireland. It's a beautiful and historic place that the English sometimes call Argyllshire. I like to imagine that the Fat Lady is taking refuge in a picturesque painting of a castle on a hilly green shore which overlooks a splendiferous blue sea. Good on the Fat Lady.

WRONG-FOOT (PAGE 169)

Oliver Wood is convinced that Slytherin is attempting to "wrong-foot" the Gryffindor team by backing out of the match and making them play Hufflepuff instead. Although Fred thinks Oliver is overreacting, Oliver's sure the Slytherin's motive is to mess with their heads, to psych them out, to mislead them, to steer them in the wrong direction … in short, to wrong-foot them. As you might expect, 'wrong-foot' has a strong familial connection with the phrase "we got off on the wrong foot," which is common in both the U.S and the U.K. (or at least it used to be) and means 'off to a bad start.'

MANGY CUR (PAGE 175)

Wow, this Sir Cadogan character is always up for a fight! This time he calls Harry a "mangy cur" and challenges him to a fight as Harry stumbles through the portrait hole on his way to breakfast. Mangy is easy. We use it to describe anything (usually an animal) with a scruffy or disgusting coat. So it fits well with the word 'cur' which refers to a lowly mixed-breed dog. Derived from the Middle English and dating back to the 13th century, cur comes from the word 'curren' which means to growl. Whatever its origins, it's a pretty rotten thing for Sir Cadogan to be calling our Harry!

– Chapter 10 –
The Marauder's Map

Chapter Summary:

Harry asks Professor Lupin to teach him to defend himself against the dementors. Later, while his friends are off at Hogsmeade, Fred and George give Harry a Christmas gift—the Maurader's Map. The magical map shows the whereabouts of each person at Hogwarts, plus secret passages to Hogsmeade. Using the map, Harry secretly joins Ron and Hermione in the village where he overhears Professor McGonagall, Hagrid and others discussing Sirius Black. It turns out that Black was Harry's father's best friend, and Harry's godfather. They say that Black betrayed Harry's parents to Voldemort, leading to their deaths, and killed their friend, Peter Pettigrew who confronted him. Black was then taken to Azkaban Prison.

SKIVING OFF (PAGE 185)

To "skive off" means to skip class or school. It's their equivalent of our 'playing hooky' and like that phrase, it *can* be used by adults to talk about skipping work or other responsibilities but it really belongs to school kids. When Ron says he's skiving off, he doesn't have to add from what. Everyone around him would understand that he's referring to class or school. Because that's the thing you skive off from.

WINDING ME UP (PAGE 192)

This is one of the milder ways in which a Brit can say, "You're kidding me." Another version would be to say, "You're taking the mick" (or mickey), which means, roughly, "You're making fun of me." Winding me up also has a sense of 'you're messing with me' as it conjures images of Jack-in-the-boxes or alarm clocks, i.e. things you wind up until they go off or explode.

MESSRS. (PAGE 192)

This is how Mooney, Wormtail, Padfoot and Prongs refer to themselves on the Marauder's Map and there's no doubt they're being ironic by putting on such formal airs.

Messrs. is a formal way to address a number of men at the same time. This goes back to the 18th century and is an abbreviation of Messieurs—which is French, I know, not English, but deal. Messieurs is the plural of monsieur which means mister, *en francaise*. So why steal from the French on this one? It seems that Mr. and Mrs. didn't form abbreviated plurals easily so the French abbreviation was adopted. For formal usage, that is.

How about addressing more than one woman? That would be with the abbreviation "Mmes."—which is short for Mesdames, which is the plural of Madame. Madame translates to our Mrs., but not exactly. Mrs. is derived from 'Mistress' and Madame originates from 'my lady.' Like Mr. comes from 'Mister' and Monsieur comes from 'my lord.'

Here are examples of using this formal plural:

Mr. Smith (singular), the Messrs. Smith (plural)

Mrs. Smith (singular), the Mmes. Smith (plural)

Be sure to address your guests with these formal titles when throwing your next high- falutin' dinner party.

NICKED (PAGE 198)

I can't believe we're this far into the books and this is the first time "nicked" has appeared. Because "to nick" is very common British slang from the 1800s that means "to steal"— but not in a grand theft auto sort of way. It's more like petty or mischievous theft as when Fred and George "nicked" the marauder's map.

A nick in the U.K. can also be slang for a police station. Where people who nick often end up.

PINTS (PAGE 202)

Hagrid's mulled mead is served in pints. Because this is how beverages (mostly beer and ale) are served in pubs. Although bottled beers are now just about as common in U.K. pubs as they are in U.S. bars, an old school patron (like Hagrid) would want something 'from the tap' or 'on draft' and would ask for a pint. Which is served in a glass. But you wouldn't ask for a glass. Just a pint. If you ask for a glass, you'll receive the smaller (and more ladylike) version, the half-pint.

But here's the mind-blowing part of this that I didn't know until now. The pint used in pubs is not the same as our pint. What?!!! In pubs, they use an Imperial Pint, which is 20 fluid ounces while over here a pint is a measly 16 fluid ounces. Now before you go thinking our American pint-sellers are duping their customers by messing with the size of a pint, you should know that *we* didn't change things— the Brits did. Before 1824, pints in both countries, as well as the countries of the British Empire, varied according to local custom (or the whims of publicans) but the most common size was the 16 ounce one. The British Weights & Measures Act of 1824 standardized the 20 ounce 'Imperial' size as the legal one throughout the Empire. But the U.S. in 1824—as you know if you've been paying attention—had been very much *not* part of the British Empire for nearly fifty years, so we stuck to our guns. Or our pint size.

Now that we've got that settled, here are a couple of examples of how to order beer in a pub. Read on if you are eighteen or older (because the drinking age in the U.K. is eighteen!)

"Hello, mate. Pint of Guiness, please." Guiness is an Irish dry stout that is almost black in color with a white foamy top that is served at room temperature. And 'mate' is a friendly way to address a male bartender.

"May I have a half of lager, love?" This means I'll have a half-pint of a paler beer which is derived from brewing at cooler temperatures. If you are from the north of England, specifically Liverpool, a man (or woman) might add a 'love' to the end of the sentence when addressing a female bartender. 'Love' is a standard form of endearment that can be said to a woman working in a shop or a restaurant and is not creepy at all. Unless an American tries it.

MULLED MEAD (PAGE 202)

It must be getting close to the end of term if Hagrid is drinking mulled mead because this is an alcoholic beverage that would be served around Christmas. The holiday version of mead is served warm and flavored with spices.

The main difference between mead and other other alcoholic beverages is that, with mead, the sugar used in the fermentation process is mostly from honey. Mead has been around since ancient times in Europe and shows up in mythology and literature from way, way back.

In Britain, mead was mentioned over a thousand years ago in Beowulf, an epic story and one of the oldest surviving pieces of Old English long form lit, which tells of warriors drinking mead.

Interestingly, monasteries—especially those monasteries engaged in bee-keeping—continued the tradition of making mead when governments placed certain restrictions around the making of alcoholic beverages like wine. Because mead was made with honey, not grapes.

TA (PAGE 202)

Upon receiving his four pints of mulled mead from Rosmerta, Hagrid offers a simple, "Ta." Ta means thank you. Informally. This usage dates back to the 18th century and started as a child's thank you. Now, "ta" is a colloquialism used by almost any Brit. But remember, it's for informal situations. Ta is what you'd say to your friends. Not to your friend's parents. And definitely not to the queen. A simple 'thank you' will still work for the likes of them.

MOTORBIKE (PAGE 206)

A Brit would rarely say motorcycle. They'd call it a motorbike—which translates to motorcycle and does not mean some kind of motorized bike or moped. Because can you imagine Hagrid trying to fit on something as small as that?!

– CHAPTER 11 –

THE FIREBOLT

CHAPTER SUMMARY:

The next day Harry wakes to find the dormitory empty except for Ron and Hermione who have decided to stay with him during the Christmas break. They warn Harry not to go after Sirius Black and remind him that when Peter Pettigrew did, all that was left of him was a finger. On Christmas morning, Harry receives an anonymous gift—a Firebolt, the best broomstick ever made. Hermione is suspicious of the gift and after Christmas dinner, she tells Professor McGonagall about it. McGonagall shows up in the Gryffindor common room and confiscates the Firebolt, saying it must be tested for jinxes. Hermione tells the angry boys that she and Professor McGonagall believe the broomstick came from Sirius Black.

MINCE PIES (PAGE 222)

In the Christmas day package from Mrs. Weasley, she's included homemade mince pies. A whole dozen of them! This is such a distinctly British thing. Mince pies are served at Christmas. But don't think our regular apple pie-sized pies. The ones Mrs. Weasley sent were individual-sized pies, like mini-pies that are made with mincemeat.

Mincemeat? That's made of meat, right? Ha! It's not. Mincemeat is what they call a mixture of spices and dried fruits and animal fats (mostly suet) mixed together and baked up in a pie pastry.

It's a somewhat sweet pie that harks back to the 13th century when Crusaders came back to Europe with recipes and ingredients acquired from the Middle East. Also called a Christmas pie, it could include such spices as nutmeg, cinnamon and cloves. And occasionally meat. Just to make things more confusing.

CHRISTMAS CRACKER (PAGE 227)

Back in *The Sorcerer's Stone* section, I took a stab at defining the "cracker" but now I realize I left out the most important part. A Christmas cracker (that long tube with two twisted ends that you pull apart at Christmas dinner, creating a small explosion and tearing the cracker in two) isn't something you tug apart on your own. It's something you do with someone else at the table, which usually devolves into a competitive tug of war. When the cracker comes apart, whoever gets the bigger end wins the goodies inside. It's sort of like pulling the wishbone, but instead of getting a wish, you get prizes, including a paper crown. In this case, Dumbledore challenges Snape to a Christmas cracker pull, and wins. We know Dumbledore wins because he's the one who puts on the witch's hat (instead of the paper crown that is the norm for Muggles' crackers) that was hiding inside the cracker. His further reward: getting to wear the silly hat on his head for the rest of Christmas dinner.

CHIPOLATAS (PAGE 230)

A common sausage in the U.K. Think the long thin kind (not a patty). Chipolatas came from France and are made from pork mixed with lots of spices and herbs. In the U.K., they're often a part of Christmas Dinner, served with the turkey. Sometimes chipolatas are festively wrapped in bacon and are then called pigs in blankets. Huh? *Our* pigs in blankets are little link sausages wrapped in biscuit dough or pastry, so I guess we'll have to chalk this one up as another unexplainable difference between us.

FLAGON (PAGE 230)

When Sir Cadogan raises his "flagon of mead," he's probably

holding up a large drinking vessel which holds two imperial pints. A flagon can be formed like a jug with one, two or three spouts. The neck of the flagon would have a ring or two for holding, and when drinking, the flagon is balanced on a raised elbow and lifted up to meet the drinker's lips. It can be made of different materials: ceramics, metal, leather or even glass and was developed for taking liquids out into the fields for refreshment when laboring. The flagon dates back to Roman times and is related to the word "flask," a smaller carry-your-beverage-with-you container that is preferred in modern times.

– CHAPTER 12 –
THE PATRONUS

CHAPTER SUMMARY:

Professor Lupin teaches Harry the Patronus charm—a kind of positive force field that keeps a dementor at bay. Lupin releases a boggart which takes the form of Harry's fear, a dementor, and on the third try Harry has some success with the charm. Harry also learns that Lupin knew his father and Sirius Black when they all attended Hogwarts. By February, Harry has made progress with the charm and Lupin tells him about the Dementor's Kiss, which is how a dementor sucks a person's soul out. It's what they will do to Black when they catch him. Harry is happily surprised when McGonagall returns his Firebolt and back in the dorm, Ron is furious with Hermione when he suspects that Crookshanks has eaten Scabbers.

SHIRTY (PAGE 244)

When Wood tells Harry that McGonagall got "shirty" with him, it's just a Brit idiom that means annoyed or angry, and more specifically the sort of annoyed or angry that isn't loud and aggressive, but snarky and bristly. You know, the kind of condescending tight-lipped anger that really makes you want to get shirty right back at them.

YEOMEN (PAGE 249)

When Sir Cadogan refers to Harry and Ron as his yeomen, he's probably being militarily specific about it. A yeoman was the third rank of fighting men in knighthood—below Knights and Squires, but above Knaves. Brits of a later vintage than Sir C (but still long before Harry's time) could often use the word more loosely to mean a fine and dutiful fellow, albeit of the lower classes. Yeoman is still a rank in the U.S. Navy, where it means an enlisted man or woman who performs primarily administrative duties.

CLAP THIS LOON IN IRONS (PAGE 249)

Well, loon's easy; Sir Cadogan is casting aspersions on Neville's mental competence. Clap someone in irons is a long standing idiom which means basically 'arrest this person.' The irons in question would be either medieval prison chains or these days, the slightly more civilized police handcuffs. Oh, and 'clap' doesn't have anything to do with applause. It's just a typically colorful Brit way of saying 'throw' or 'place.' It also implies an imperative to do it quickly, which suggests that the origin of the metaphorical usage might be from 'clap of thunder' because thunder isn't just loud but also sudden and unexpected.

ODDSBODIKINS (PAGE 249)

The password that Harry gets right so they can enter Gryffindor Tower. 'Oddsbodikins' is a very old euphemism for a medieval curse or oath, 'God's Body,' which was considered too blasphemous to be used in polite company. Unlike 'Cor Blimey' which is a direct contraction of 'God Blind Me,' Odds Bodikins (as it was more commonly spelled) was just a sound alike replacement. Interestingly, 'bodkin' was a real word back then, and was the name of a small tool used for making holes in leather.

– CHAPTER 13 –
GRYFFINDOR VERSUS RAVENCLAW

CHAPTER SUMMARY:

The incident with Scabbers puts Ron and Hermione at odds. Harry flies on his amazing Firebolt at Quidditch practice and then thinks he sees the eyes of the Grim—which turns out to be Crookshanks. At the Gryffindor vs. Ravenclaw match, Harry finds their seeker, Cho Chang, to be both pretty and a worthy adversary. As he goes after the Golden Snitch, Harry spots three dementors on the pitch below and conjures a Patronus charm. After catching the snitch and winning the game, Harry discovers that the "dementors" were Malfoy and his friends dressed in black robes and hoods. That night, Harry is awakened by Ron's scream. Turns out Sirius Black had come to Ron's bed, holding a knife. But now Black is gone.

NO NEW ENTRIES.

– CHAPTER 14 –
SNAPE'S GRUDGE

CHAPTER SUMMARY:

There is a search for Black but he has escaped. On Saturday, Harry, with his invisibility cloak in tow, joins Ron in Hogsmeade. When Malfoy, Crabbe and Goyle taunt Ron outside the Shrieking Shack, invisible Harry plays tricks on them. But his cloak slips and they see him. Harry hurries back to Hogwarts but is caught by Snape and taken to his office where Harry discovers that Snape has a grudge against his father. Snape seizes the Maurader's Map and calls in Lupin. When Lupin leaves with Ron and Harry—and the map—he chastises Harry for putting himself in danger. Back at the common room, Hermione informs them that Hagrid did not win Buckbeak's case and that the Hippogriff will be put to death.

CHEERS (PAGE 272)

Like "ta," this is another Brit-way to say 'thanks.' Informally, that is. It's also used as a way to say hello or goodbye and as a sign off in letters or emails, as Hagrid does here. By closing his short note with "Cheers, Hagrid," he's really combining the goodness of sincerely and thanks, rolled together in one handy catchall word.

My English husband says cheers all the time, like the Brit he is, using it mostly for thanks or goodbyes. I'm used to it now, but for a long time it sounded weird to me because I grew up hearing "cheers" only as a toast—you know, with glasses raised and that sort of thing. Well, the Brits use it for that too, but take note—if a modern Brit says cheers to you, the likelihood is that he or she is not giving a drink-less toast, but is just saying hi, saying bye or offering his or her thanks.

BATH BUNS (PAGE 273)

A bath bun, when not baked by Hagrid, should be delicious. Created in the English city of Bath, the Bath bun dates back to the 18th century. It's a sweet roll made with a yeast dough that's dressed up with a topping of candied fruit or sprinkled sugar or both. Sometimes the buns would be baked with a lump of sugar buried inside. This lovely sweet bread reached a kind of zenith when a million of them were baked and eaten over the five and a half months of the Great Exhibition of 1851 which was held in London's Hyde Park. During this period, they became known as the "London Bath bun," which is as odd as a Chicago Boston Cream Pie.

HIGH STREET (PAGE 278)

When Harry and Ron head toward the High Street in Hogsmeade, it just means they are going to the main drag of the town or what we might call the Main Street. And just like many main streets in American towns aren't actually called Main Street (though most are), every high street in the U.K. isn't necessarily called High Street (though many—like the one in Hogsmeade—are). Idiomatically, though, whether the street in question is actually named High Street or not, Brits will often call it that informally.

MASTER OF THIS SCHOOL (P. 286)

When Snape threatens the Marauder's Map, calling himself "master of this school," he doesn't mean he's *the* master—he isn't planning a secret coup against Dumbledore's authority or anything. Teachers in British schools are also called masters (or mistresses), which is why the head teacher is called the Headmaster (or Headmistress).

– CHAPTER 15 –
THE QUIDDITCH FINAL

CHAPTER SUMMARY:
After the news about Buckbeak, Hermione apologizes to Ron for what happened to Scabbers and they make up. When Malfoy makes fun of Hagrid for being emotional about Buckbeak, Hermione smacks Malfoy across the face and draws her wand on him. Then, in Divination class, Hermione has words with Madam Trelawney, calls it quits, and storms out of the classroom. The night before the Quidditch Final, Harry sees a huge black dog on the grounds beneath his window. During the match, the Slytherins play dirty and rack up many penalties trying to beat Gryffindor. Finally, Harry grabs the Golden Snitch (almost out of the hands of Slytherin seeker, Malfoy) and Gryffindor wins the Quidditch Cup!

DODDERY (PAGE 292)
Hermione describes the members of the committee that has sentenced Buckbeak to death as "doddery," which is a word that isn't exclusively British—it's technically part of American English, too—but it's certainly much more commonly used over there. Strictly speaking, it's merely descriptive, referring to someone or something that is unsteady in movement. But nine times out of ten, it's used as an insult aimed primarily at old people and sometimes at not-so-old people who you want to offend by suggesting they're old and weak and wobbly. Those Brits. Not always as charming as you think, huh?

FLIBBERTIGIBBET (PAGE 295)

The Fat Lady is back and this is the password that Ron and Harry have to use to get into Gryffindor tower. Meaning a frivolous, chattery, scatterbrained person, it dates from Medieval times and was an onomatopoeic construct intended to sound like a babbled bunch of nonsense syllables. Because it was a made-up word, there were many variant spellings for hundreds of years—flepergebet, flibber de jib, flipperty-gibbet—but Shakespeare spelled it 'Flibbertigibbet' in *King Lear* so that might be the reason this spelling was the one that stuck (even though Shakespeare was a terrible—or, to be kind, inconsistent—speller). The place you're most likely to have heard the word in modern times is in the lyric to "How Do You Solve a Problem Like Maria?", a song from *The Sound of Music*.

BOTTLEBRUSH TAIL (PAGE 303)

It turns out that Hermione's cat Crookshanks has a bottlebrush tail, which *sounds* like the kind of phrase J. K. Rowling likes to invent but in fact has been around for many many years (and is used here as well as in the U.K.). It's purely—and perfectly—descriptive and refers to those feline tails that aren't smooth-lying and sleek but instead look *exactly* like the kind of long stiff-but-bushy cleaning brushes that are used to get inside bottles, beakers, or tall thin glasses.

– CHAPTER 16 –
PROFESSOR TRELAWNEY'S PREDICTION

CHAPTER SUMMARY:

Harry does well on his Defense Against the Dark Arts exam but his Divination one-on-one with Madam Trelawney ends with the professor going into a sort of trance, saying that before midnight Lord Voldemort's servant will join him again and help him return to power. After the exam, Harry gets the bad news that Buckbeak's appeal was lost and that the Hippogriff will be put to death at sunset. Harry, Ron and Hermione hurry to Hagrid's hut where Hermione finds Ron's rat in a milk jug. As Dumbledore, Fudge and an executioner approach, Harry, Ron and Hermione sneak out the backdoor, passing Buckbeak who is tied up in the pumpkin patch. Before they reach the castle, they hear the sound of an axe falling.

MEDIEVAL WITCH HUNTS (PAGE 318)
(See the entry for *witch burning* in chapter one of this section)

PADDLING POOL (PAGE 318)
What we call a baby pool or kiddie pool. An inflatable, above ground, backyard pool.

– CHAPTER 17 –
CAT, RAT, AND DOG

CHAPTER SUMMARY:

On the way back to the castle, Scabbers wriggles out of Ron's hands. After Ron catches the rat, they see a huge black dog. The dog pounces on Harry, then drags Ron through the hole at the bottom of the Whomping Willow tree, breaking Ron's leg. Harry and Hermione go after them, through the long tunnel which leads to the Shrieking Shack. There they find Ron and Sirius Black. We discover that Black is an Animagus, a person who can take the form of an animal—in Black's case, a huge dog. Harry tries to attack Black, then Lupin arrives, having found them using the Marauder's Map. After an exchange, Lupin hugs Black and says there's another Animagus in the room and that Scabbers is really Peter Pettigrew.

NO NEW ENTRIES.

– CHAPTER 18 –
MOONY, WORMTAIL, PADFOOT, AND PRONGS

CHAPTER SUMMARY:

Lupin believed that Peter was dead until he saw him in the Marauder's Map. As Scabbers struggles to get free from Ron's grasp, Lupin explains it all started when he became best friends with Sirius, Peter and Harry's father, James when they were students at Hogwarts. The friends secretly became Animagi so they could join Lupin when he was a werewolf in the Shrieking Shack without coming to harm. Their nicknames were Moony, Wormtail, Padfoot and Prongs and they drew up the Marauder's map. Lupin says that Professor Snape doesn't trust him because of a trick Sirius played on Snape in their student days. Suddenly, Snape reveals himself from under Harry's invisibility cloak and aims his wand at Lupin.

NO NEW ENTRIES.

– CHAPTER 19 –
THE SERVANT OF LORD VOLDEMORT

CHAPTER SUMMARY:

Convinced that Lupin has been helping Black, Snape magically bounds Lupin, then turns his wand toward Black. Hermione and Ron disarm Snape and he falls unconscious to the floor. Black tells them that it was Peter who betrayed Harry's parents and killed all those Muggles twelve years ago. Peter faked his own death and pinned the murders on Black. When Black realized that Peter was alive and at Hogwarts, he escaped from prison to protect Harry. Lupin and Black turn the rat back into Peter Pettigrew and Peter confesses to being Voldemort's spy. Harry stops Lupin and Black from killing him, saying his father wouldn't want his friends to be murderers. He thinks it would be better for Pettigrew to go to Azkaban.

NO NEW ENTRIES.

– Chapter 20 –
The Dementor's Kiss

Chapter Summary:

Returning through the tunnel, Black asks Harry to come live with him when he is free. When they emerge back on school grounds, the moon appears and Lupin turns into a werewolf. Black changes into a dog, attacking Lupin to protect the others. Meanwhile, Pettigrew transforms into a rat and escapes. When Harry and Hermione hear a dog's yelp in the distance, they find Black (as a man again) by the lake with dementors approaching. But Harry cannot produce a Patronus powerful enough to ward them off. Harry is about to receive the Dementor's kiss when the dementors unexpectedly retreat. Before he passes out, Harry sees a gleaming animal on the lake and a familiar looking person on the other shore.

No new entries.

– CHAPTER 21 –
HERMIONE'S SECRET

CHAPTER SUMMARY:

In the hospital wing, Harry learns that Snape found them by the lake and brought them to the castle and that Sirius has been locked up, awaiting the Dementor's kiss. Dumbledore believes Harry and Hermione when they say that Black is innocent but says no one else will. The only way to rescue Sirius is to use the Time-Turner around Hermione's neck, what she's used through the year to attend her simultaneous classes. Going back three hours, Harry and Hermione first save Buckbeak. Then, at the lake, Harry produces a Patronus—in a form of a stag—that drives the dementors away and saves their former selves. Flying on Buckbeak, Harry and Hermione rescue Sirius and watch Sirius and Buckbeak escape into the night sky.

WAISTCOAT (P. 391)

I find it hard to believe this is the first time that waistcoat has shown up in the books because I'm sure many adult men wear waistcoats in Potter world. A waistcoat is simply what we call a vest and was once the common third element in a tailored men's suit. It was where men like Minister Fudge would have a pocket watch stashed... in say, 1920.

– CHAPTER 22 –
OWL POST AGAIN

CHAPTER SUMMARY:

Harry and Hermione make it back to the hospital wing just as the three hours are up and tell Dumbledore of their success. The next day, Harry, Ron and Hermione find out that Lupin has resigned believing it's safer for the students if he leaves, and Lupin returns the Marauder's Map to Harry. Harry is saddened by Lupin leaving, the prospect of Pettigrew returning to Voldemort and his returning to the Dursleys. Things improve on the Hogwarts Express when Harry receives an owl post from Sirius, which includes a Hogsmeade permission slip for next year. Harry is met by his Uncle Vernon at King's Cross Station but he's already looking ahead to when he'll go to the Quidditch World Cup with the Weasleys during the summer.

N.E.W.T.s (PAGE 430)

N.E.W.T.s are the subject-specific exams Hogwarts pupils take at the end of their seventh year, just like Muggles take A-Levels at the end of *their* seventh year (or the second year of their Sixth Form, aka Upper Sixth). Remember we learned about Muggle O-levels and Wizard O.W.L.s (the subject-specific exams taken at the end of the fifth year) when we talked about them in *Chamber of Secrets*? A-levels (and Newts, or Nastily Exhausting Wizard Tests) are the last exams of secondary school and help determine which Universities you might go to or which career you might start.

Interestingly, this isn't the first time that Newts and Owls have been associated together with literary witches and wizards. In Shakespeare's *Macbeth*, the three witches' rhyming spell (the beginning of which is famously misremembered as "hubble, bubble, toil and trouble" but is actually "double, double, toil and trouble"), includes a whole list of very unsavory ingredients that the ladies are throwing into their cauldron. Among those ingredients are 'eye of newt' and 'owlet's wing.' Before you get too grossed out, you should know that most of the disgusting words or phrases are actually just old folk-terms for herbs or plants. Eye of Newt, for example, is simply Mustard Seed.

TEA CART (PAGE 431)

How fitting that the last entry in this book about Britishness is once again related to that most British of beverages, tea. Remember almost three years ago when Ron bought the chocolate frog from the lady with the candy cart in *Sorcerer's Stone*? Well, the "tea cart" is a very real thing on trains and has been part of rail travel in the U.K. for a century. You know when the flight attendants wheel a cart up the aisle on a plane? Its origin was the rail-based tea cart. Although the modern railways' catering trolley also offers snacks and many other beverages, it's always called a tea cart. Because, as we have learned, the most important thing in the world for any self-respecting Brit is a nice cup of tea.

INDEX

Lounge, 115
Love from, 128
Lovely, 128

- M -
Mad, 33
Magnolia Crescent, 203
Majorca, 33
Mangy cur, 240
Manor, 124
Marks, 51
Marmalade, 46
Mars bars, 73
Master, 129
Master of this School, 256
Me, 56
Medieval, 161
Medieval Witch Hunts, 259
Mental, 231
Merlin, 52
Meself, 50
Messrs., 242
Milk bottles, 30
Mince pies, 247
Mind, 50
Minister, 61
Ministry, 61
Monk, 79
Moors, 134
Morgana, 74
Motorbike, 245
Mulled mead, 244

Mum, 51
Mummy, 34
Musical statues, 198
Must get on, 63

- N -
N.E.W.T.s, 271
National squad, 164
Nicked, 242
Nicolas Flamel, 73
Nightcap, 165
Nightdress, 125
Nightshirt, 213
Nip, 142
Norfolk, 135
Nosh, 200
Number 4 Privet Drive, 15
Nun, 150
Nutter, 224

- O -
O.W.L.s, 128
Oddsbodikins, 252
Old boy, 215
Ottery St. Catchpole, 124
Oy, 71

- P -
Paddington Station, 67
Paddling pool, 259
Palmistry, 218
Parcel, 32

Coming Soon...

THE
YOUNG
AMERICAN'S
UNOFFICIAL
GUIDE TO THE
VERY
BRITISH
WORLD
OF

Harry Potter

VOLUME
TWO

DANA MIDDLETON

Dana Middleton is a producer of an Academy Award-nominated short film and is a recipient of a Los Angeles Theatre Ovation Award. She lives in sunny Los Angeles with her British husband, writes books for children, and is a huge fan of the Harry Potter series.

shadowridgepress.com

Made in the USA
Middletown, DE
13 September 2021